A Sparrow Falls

Lynda Shelhamer

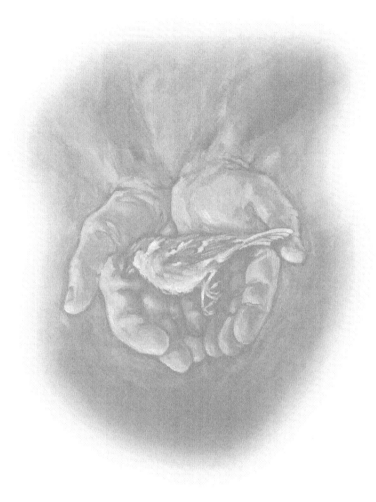

© Cover by Lois Rosio Sprague: LoisRosioSprague.com
© Cover Image: image copyright
© Inside illustrations by Lynda Shelhamer

And yet not one sparrow falls to the ground
apart from your Father knowing it.

Matthew 10:29

Dedicated to:

Josiah Wesley Shelhamer

Whose death defined the rest of my life in so many ways.

I miss smelling your softness, feeling the tears that you were
unable to cry, groping for the answers to your deep and difficult
questions and ... cuddling till you laughed ... cuddling ...

1983 - 1998

Contents

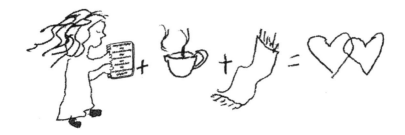

Introduction

This practical "hands on" journal is for moms whose sparrow has fallen, yet not to the ground ... but into Jesus' nail-pierced hands.

The Japanese have a saying: "a mother buries her parents on the mountain, but her children in her heart."

Having lost my precious fifteen year old son to a self-inflicted gunshot wound, I hurt with you! We are fellow "wounded warriors" slogging through the horrific valley known as GRIEF.

Is there such a thing as "good grief" Charlie Brown? I contend there is, but it takes work on our part. There are libraries full of wonderful books on grief and mothers' stories. This devotional, however, is meant for the mom who is too fatigued or unable to focus on an entire book. It is a collection of short, one-day devotionals that are filled with hope. The intent is to have your sparrow teach you how to fly and sing again!

So, whether you are a mom whose "sparrow has fallen" from miscarriage, murder or medical causes, drowning or drug overdose, suicide, stillborn or sudden death, grab a cup of hot coffee or tea, a snuggly blanket and let's share heart-to-heart!

It was a year before I met *another mom* who had experienced the nightmare I had and, when we finally connected, we couldn't quit talking! With social media and the Internet that may not be true for you, however here's your chance to connect with yet *another mom.*

Each devotional will guide you into words from:
- A mom's heart
- Your Father's heart
- And, should you choose, words from *your* heart.

Feel free to:
- Doodle or scribble wildly in the margins
- Throw the journal down
- Or grasp it to your heart!

The ~*Heavenly Hope*~ section of each chapter is intended as a dialogue between you and your God or can be used as a springboard for discussion with a spouse or favorite chick friend.

Though some Scripture verses are written out for you, others are not. This is my attempt to challenge you to actually look up a Bible verse for yourself. I am a Bible Study Nerd and I want you to become one too! Romans 15:4, "*... so that through perseverance and the encouragement of the Scriptures we might have hope."*

My prayer for you is that you will find *treasures in your darkness,* as I have and that the Man of Sorrows Himself will bind and *heal* your *broken heart.*

Treasures in the Darkness

I will give you the treasures of darkness
and hidden wealth of secret places, so that you may know
that it is I the Lord who calls you by name.
Isaiah 45:3

My kids loved treasure hunts and I loved creating them! Ten spring-time clues led to a concealed Easter Basket. "Gold Rush Days" in the summer found the kids scurrying around the yard on an eager search for painted gold rocks. One memorable camping trip at the beach, we read *Treasure Island* and buried a treasure chest under the sandy shoreline.

When I stepped into the Black Abyss of Grief, God whispered to me the first clue: "Treasures will be found in the darkness!"

Finding a treasure requires a map, eagerness (well, at least enough energy to sit up in bed), persistence and a few tools. God has given us His Word as a Treasure Map. *A Sparrow Falls* is meant to give you a few tools that I have used to find "treasures in your darkness."

Did you know that in New Zealand there are actually Glow Worm Caves? Yes, glowworms do exist outside of the song "Glow Little Glow Worm, Glimmer, Glimmer." However, their beautiful strange light can only be seen in the pitch darkness of caves and jungle like areas. Stars and planets are best seen on the darkest nights in the darkest regions of earth. Diamonds displayed on black velvet will showcase their brightest brilliance! There are nuggets/truths that only show up in the dark. Take advantage of this strange journey you are on; the jewels you will find are rare gems!

My prayer for you is that, as you search for these jewels in the dark crevices of grief you will experience what God also promises in this verse: *"... so that you will know that it is I the Lord who calls you by your NAME."*

Put on your night vision glasses and for the next 40 days, Mom, your name is *Treasure Hunter.*

... because of the tender mercy of our God with which the Sunrise from on high will visit us to shine upon those who sit in darkness and the shadow of death to guide our feet into the way of peace.
Luke 1:78-79

Who promises to sit with us in our darkness and our shadow of death?

What is His purpose for sitting with us there?

What can illuminate the path for people walking in darkness?
(Isaiah 9:2; II Samuel 22:29, 30; Psalm 119:105)

Tears in a Bottle

You keep track of all my sorrows.
You have collected all my tears in Your bottle.
You have recorded each one in Your book.
Psalm 56:8

Under a microscope, tears of laughter look completely different than tears of grief (see pictures at www.lifebuzz.com/tears/).

At Rose-Lyn Fisher's website she states: "What is perhaps most intriguing are all the different forms tears take, depending on the emotions behind them. Tears of laughter, tears of grief and onion tears, all look remarkably different." They even have different saline and protein levels!

God hasn't put our tears under a microscope but He has put them in a bottle and recorded each tear in a book!

Often in the Scriptures it says that God hears our cries. Think about it – the God of Creation is encompassed by the sounds of heaven; sounds that have been described as the sounds of many waters, thunderous, continual praise permeating His throne room. Suddenly He pauses and tunes into my weeping in my little bedroom! *In my distress I called to the Lord; I called out to my God. From His Temple he heard my voice and my cry came to His ears.* (II Samuel 22:7) Amazing! He not only hears our cries and sees our tears but He puts each tear in a bottle and records them in a book!

What size bottle does God need to hold your tears?

My personal bottle cracked as the tears became a river, then an ocean, recorded in a book or scroll (as it is translated) that rolled out ad-infinitum. Believe me sisters; we don't have the last chapter!

The point is our tears are like precious ointment to Him. They are worth saving, like the precious ointment Mary had in the bottle that she used to wash Jesus' feet. Let your tears flow, filling God's coveted bottle!

Heavenly Hope

For the Lamb Who is in the midst of the throne will shepherd them and lead them to the living fountain of water and God will wipe away every tear from their eyes. Revelation 7:17

If God goes to all this trouble to hear, see and record our tears, why doesn't He just prevent them in the first place?

How does it feel to you that the God of Creation is hearing your cries?

What do you think it means to sow with tears? (Psalm 126:5)

My mother wiped my tears and my father told me to buck up. Not your heavenly Father – look! (Isaiah 25:8 & 9)

_____

_____

_____

_____

_____

_____

_____

_____

_____

_____

_____

_____

Mary's Perfume

Mary took a pound of very costly perfume of pure nard
and anointed the feet of Jesus and wiped His feet with her hair;
and the house was filled with the fragrance of the perfume.
John 12:3

Touring the King Tutankhamen exhibit, the beauty of an Egyptian alabaster perfume bottle struck me. The colors of the translucent stone bottle danced and played under the display lights. Such was the bottle that held Mary's precious perfume worth a *year's wage*. Had she scrimped, sacrificed and saved to purchase this ointment? Yet the Bible portrays her in the Gospels of John and Mark, breaking the beautiful vial and pouring it on Jesus' head and dusty feet. When the vial was broken the beautiful fragrance filled the room.

Now, if God had asked of me to offer cheap cologne (used to be referred to as "toilette water") or even my $100 bottle of Chanel, that would have been easy! I'd readily break the vial and give it to Him.

"But Lord? The broken body of my child pouring out his lifeblood for a bigger picture?" Tear-infused perfume!

Mary didn't know the bigger picture as she held the beautiful broken shards in her hand. Jesus explained that she had anointed Him for his burial. That very week His own body would be broken on the cross and His lifeblood poured to the ground, filling the world with its fragrance!

Judas and the others were standing around calling Mary's sacrifice "a waste" (John 12:4-6, Mark 14:4). Satan wants you to believe that your child's death was a total waste. It's not, moms! What's poured out at Jesus' feet can fill a room with its fragrance.

While He was in Bethany at the home of Simon the leper and reclining at the table, there came a woman with an alabaster vial of very costly perfume of pure nard; and she broke the vial and poured it over His head. But some were indignantly remarking to one another, "Why has this perfume been wasted? For this perfume might have been sold for over three hundred denarii and the money given to the poor." And they were scolding her. But Jesus said, "Let her alone; why do you bother her? She has done a good deed to Me. For you always have the poor with you and whenever you wish you can do good to them; but you do not always have Me. She has done what she could; she has anointed My body beforehand for the burial. Truly I say to you, wherever the gospel is preached in the whole world, what this woman has done will also be spoken of in memory of her." Mark 14:3-9

Even though it feels like a "total waste," can you retain the hope of the broken shards of your child's death someday having value and giving off a fragrance?

How can the aroma of your child's death become an aroma of life?
(II Corinthians 2:14-15, Ephesians 5:1, 2)

_____

_____

_____

_____

_____

Loosened Sackcloth

You have turned my mourning into dancing,
You have loosed my sackcloth and
girded me with gladness.
Psalm 30:11

One Old Testament Jewish grieving tradition was to don sackcloth and place ashes on one's head. Sackcloth was a coarse black cloth made from goat's hide. It was worn to symbolize one's deep personal mourning and loss. It often caused rashes and itching. Job *covered* himself in sackcloth!

Now, I'll admit to possessing a few uncomfortable garments in lieu of vanity. But give me a black dress; I'm not wearing sackcloth!

Many of you reading this are in the itchy, uncomfortable, "get me out of this sackcloth" stage! I want you to see God's promise to you: Joy will come to you in the <u>mourning</u>.

I find it interesting that the Scripture doesn't say that our sackcloth is removed but loosened. We will always carry scraps of sackcloth, in memory of our child's death. But God will loosen and make it more comfortable and someday exchange it for a garment of praise!

Heavenly Hope

You have turned my mourning into dancing; You have loosed my sackcloth and girded me with gladness. Psalm 30:11

Eventually what will God exchange for your sackcloth?

Can you believe in your heart that this will someday be true?

How else is God going to clothe us? (Isaiah 61:10)

What did Daniel do while sitting in sackcloth and ashes?
(Daniel 9:3, 4)

_____

_____

_____

_____

_____

_____

_____

_____

_____

_____

_____

_____

_____

_____

_____

_____

_____

_____

_____

_____

Ground Zero

The cords of death encompassed me;
the TERRORS of Sheol came upon me.
I found distress and sorrow.
Psalm 116:3

Many horrific terms have been used to describe the moment you got the phone call, or the diagnosis, witnessed the scene or the blood.

> Night of Nightmares
> The Crash Site
> Ground Zero
> Moment of Terror

Sitting on the beach this morning, my husband recounted from his journal the moment he heard our precious Josiah was gone from a self-inflicted gunshot wound. He was fogged in at an airport when he had a strong urge to call home. When I told him, "Josiah killed himself," the coffee cup in his hand dropped to the ground, shattering and splattering hot coffee on his slacks and feet. Police arrived to escort him, sobbing, to a private area. Eighteen years later I hear the story for the first time and we cry together.

Though never being a journalist I, too, found a need to record every gory detail of that scene.

The details of the moment of terror are SO BIG inside us that we continue to mull them over in a schizophrenic confusion of wanting desperately to forget them and yet wanting to never lose them. Frequently we find ourselves visiting them over and over again.

Martin Luther said, "Satan hates a writing pen." In getting those details out where I could look at them, I felt they were a little less big inside of me. Besides, you never know when eighteen years down the road you may be sitting on a beach, sharing it with someone and finding a deeper level of love and discovery.

Heavenly Hope

"You will not be afraid of the terror by night." Psalm 91:5

The word "terror" is in the Bible 58 times. God does not say the terror will not come. But what does He say about it?

What's a good *shout* when you are feeling terror?
(Psalm 116:3-9)

Don't be afraid to look at your terror. *Consider journaling your "Ground Zero" moment.*

_____

_____

_____

_____

_____

_____

_____

_____

_____

_____

_____

_____

_____

_____

Victim or Victor?

This is the victory that overcomes the world, even our faith.
I John 5:4

Well into my grief journey, there came a moment of clarity when I knew I was given a choice: *Define* the rest of my life by my son's death, or make my son's death *my defining moment.*

There are many examples of Bible characters being offered a *defining* moment. Abraham offering his son on an altar. Esther laying her life on the line "for such a time as this." Three Hebrew slaves choosing the fiery furnace over bowing to an idol. Joseph fleeing the seduction of Potiphar's wife. All were hard choices that altered history.

Life will always be divided by "before Josiah died" (BJD) and "after Josiah died" (AJD). However I *choose* not to live the rest of my life blaming God, expecting others to walk on egg shells around me, making friend and family time all about me or savoring a *victim* mentality.

I can honor Josiah's death by being a *victor* and making his death one of my defining moments. Our pastor says, "You can't be an overcomer if you haven't been an under-wenter."

When I get to heaven and see my son again I want to be able to tell him, "I allowed God to use your death to bring about a mountain of good and godly fruit in my life and in the lives of everyone I met."

Heavenly Hope

He who overcomes will be clothed in white garments and I will not erase his name from the book of LIFE. Revelation 3:5

Look at the reward for being an overcomer!

This is the victory that overcomes the world, even our faith ...
I John 5:4, 5

What can help you be an overcomer?

What are other rewards for being an overcomer and living in victory? (Rev 2:7, 11, 17; I Corinthians 15:54, 55)

_____

_____

_____

_____

_____

_____

_____

_____

_____

_____

_____

_____

_____

_____

_____

_____

_____

_____

My Upside Down World

For indeed in this house we groan,
longing to be clothed with our dwelling from heaven.
2 Corinthians 5:2

Do you feel like you've been transported to some lost planet where nothing looks or feels familiar? I had written in my journal: "Who am I? Where am I? Friends who used to amuse me, now I find irritating and annoying. My sleep patterns are totally out of synch with time. Is there time here? I have *spatial confusion*. I have a foot on the stairs and can't remember if I'm going up them or down."

Frequently I'd question where I'm driving to and why. When I got there I would lose my car in the parking lot. (Okay, I still do that!) Lost, lost, everything lost.

Josiah, my son, identified with this alien feeling. He had stickers and a shirt that said: "Alien." In fact the night he died he tore a page out of my Bible and highlighted the following verses: Hebrews 11:13-16

> *All died in faith without receiving the promises ... having confessed that they were strangers and aliens on the earth. Those who say such things make it clear they are seeking a country of their own ... they desire a better country, that is, a heavenly one. Therefore God is not ashamed to be called their God, for He has prepared a city for them.*

We inscribed this verse on his gravestone: "He was looking for a better country, a heavenly one." (Notice that those who are seeking a heavenly country, God is not ashamed of them!)

The journey of grief that psychology describes sounds so cut and dry: Denial – Anger – Bargaining – Depression – Acceptance. But in real grief it's all scrambled – inside, outside, upside, down side. Scrambled all the time.

The truth is: this world should not fit. Randy Alcorn, in his book *Heaven*, describes this world as: "An uncomfortable garment that never feels that it fits just right and when we get to heaven, clothed in the righteousness of God we'll go 'Ah ... this fits just right!'"

Perhaps death just accentuates our irritability and uncomfortableness with this planet. Paul describes his body as a temporary dwelling place that will one day be torn down. Peter describes Christians as aliens and strangers, foreigners, pilgrims and sojourners in this world.

Can we use this "out of place" feeling to increase our faith and longing for a "better place" where our King reigns over the perfectly fitting kingdom?

Nothing's right, everything's wrong
I live in a world where nothing belongs
What once was here now is there
What once was round now is square
North is South, East is West
Time cycles gone, I no longer rest...
Nothing's right, everything's wrong

Lynda, July 1999

The Israelites wandered around *lost* in the wilderness for 40 years. They ate a strange unfamiliar food: manna. The word "manna" actually means, "What is it?" They longed for the leeks and onions of Egypt.

He humbled you, causing you to hunger and then feeding you with manna, which neither you nor your ancestors had known, to teach you that man does not live on bread alone but on every word that comes from the mouth of the Lord! Deuteronomy 8:3

What was God's purpose in this? Are you learning to feed on the Word of the Lord? As you read, ask God to feed your soul with His heavenly manna, the Bread of Life.

How does Hebrews 11:37-40 describe some of the "aliens" in the Bible?

_____

_____

_____

_____

_____

_____

_____

_____

_____

_____

_____

_____

_____

Anger – Where Do I Put It?

Be angry and sin not.
Ephesians 4:26

Anger is normal, healthy (well, can be healthy) and inevitable. Mine was a confused and convoluted anger. Confused because I grew up in a "good" Christian home where anger was seldom demonstrated or tolerated. Convoluted because Josiah was a "victim" of suicide and how can one get mad at the victim? One can be angry with an evil perpetrator, but not the victim.

One day my suppressed anger raised its ugly head with full force. Two of the siblings were acting out with unhealthy lifestyle choices. I was driving around totally lost and confused. This had now become my DMO – daily method of operation.

Pulling over, I started to sob. Pounding the steering wheel, I screamed, "I hate you Josiah! You shot us all and left us all bleeding! Why? You had it better than 99.9% of the children in the world! I hate you, I hate you, I hate you!"

Of course, I didn't hate him. I loved him deeply and thus the deep anger over his absence.

I was surprised how much better I felt after my explosive tantrum. The tears felt more cleansing than angry. I realized my anger needed to get out where I could look at it, feel it and eventually deal with it.

Though anger can be displaced onto many other people and objects, ultimately our anger is at God. He is the only One who could have prevented our child's death and He chose not to prevent it.

Some moms remain estranged from and angry with God their entire lives, but He is the only One who can help us, and He IS choosing to do just that, if we seek Him.

Heavenly Hope

Jonah 4:1-3. Jonah is displeased and suicidal. God asks him (and us), "Do you have a good reason to be angry?" Jonah doesn't answer God. God again asks Jonah the same question in verse 9. This time Jonah answers with essentially, "You're darn right I'm angry!" He then states his case for his anger and how he judges the situation as unfair. It is at that point, not before, that God ministers to Jonah.

Will you allow yourself to be honest with God about your anger?

State your case to God. Put it in writing. Allow God to minister to you.

Meditate on these verses and write down your thoughts:
(Psalm 51:6; Ecclesiastes 3:4)

_____

_____

_____

_____

_____

_____

_____

_____

_____

Just Breathe

He will not allow me to get my breath
but saturates me with bitterness.
Job 9:18

How can emotional pain feel so physical?

Hugging my Australian Shepherd, I sobbed until I felt like throwing up! She licked my hand and seemingly understood. No one warned me grieving could feel *so physical*. Dry heaves in the bathroom, desperately trying to get the horror inside out to where I could see it and all its ugly mess.

Breathing is a process that should come naturally, right? Now it took some focus! I would often find myself sitting with a close friend repeating details (aware that I was repeating details!) when suddenly I'd realize I wasn't breathing. I'd have to pause, consciously take a breath, and resume my sad story.

Frequently my goals for the day were 1) get out of bed; 2) take a step; 3) breathe. And even at that I was setting the bar pretty high!

It was my first AJD Christmas (After Josiah's Death). The song played on the radio "Breath of Heaven ... Hold Me Together" by Sandy Patty. I began to call on the Breath-Giver to be my breath when I lost mine – to hold me together when I fell apart, to lighten my darkness, as the song said.

Heavenly Hope

A verse I relied on a lot – and I still rely on – is Colossians 1:17: "He is before *all things* and in Him *all things* hold together."

Are your marriage, your family and your sanity falling apart? Call on Him right now for the "*all things*" that you need Him to hold together! What are they?

When you are paralyzed and can't take the first step out of bed, claim Acts 17:28: "In Him we *live* and *move* and *have our being*."

Great verses on losing and gaining one's breath:
(Daniel 10:17-19; Genesis 2:7)

_____

_____

_____

_____

_____

_____

_____

_____

_____

_____

_____

_____

_____

_____

_____

_____

The Grand Canyon

*When he falls he will not be hurled headlong because
the Lord is the One who holds his hand.*
Psalm 37:24

Shortly after our son died, it was spring break. We needed to go some-place where nobody knew our names or our story.

We loaded the car with a tent and the three kids and headed off to the Grand Canyon. To this day I don't know how we convinced a 12-year-old and two teenagers to hike into the depths of the canyon, but we did.

We got up while it was still dark; with snow on our tents and on the ground we began our descent. Not bad, we thought, as the yellow sun-rise illuminated the red orange canyon walls. It felt so good to be out of our house, out of our town and in the fresh air where nature gave us a bigger picture of life.

Then we turned around.

Getting back was another story altogether. The steep canyon wall looked so large and the top looked so far away. We had blissfully ig-nored the warning signs regarding the number of people who have died in the canyon and suddenly we felt we were going to up that number by five!

The arduous climb from Indian Garden pushed each of us beyond our known capabilities. I had five vertical miles to think about how much this was like grief – a long, hard climb, one step at a time with no other way out.

Having to focus on just breathing kept us from communicating with one another. We were very much aware that the only way to conquer the path out of the canyon was by putting one foot in front of the other. Getting to the next switchback might require being pushed from behind or pulled up by someone above. Back and forth, pausing to refresh and recover before attempting the next section.

Some more agile and fit hikers would pass us, accentuating our slow journey. Others walked by with encouraging words and acknowledged with empathy how tough this really was.

Everyone on the trail had the same goal: get out of this canyon before the dark and cold swallowed us up!

At one point my daughter, Amber, turned to me and said, "I can't do this mom!" I replied, "We don't have a choice. We either take the next step or die in this canyon."

So it is with grief. We really don't have a choice. It is tough. It is hard. The top looks so far away. But just keep heading to that next switchback.

While experiencing the most amazing sunset we *neared* the top. Seasoned passersby encouraged us, "You're almost there." Eventually all five of us collapsed exhausted on the South Rim.

I remember thinking there should be people with signs that say, "Hooray You Made It!" or "Good Job!" but there weren't. What *was* there was a renewed hope of maybe after being hurled into this deep chasm of grief, there was indeed a top where I would peacefully sleep again under the stars – cold snow gone!

Heavenly Hope

The Psalms have what are called "Psalms of Ascent," also known as "Songs for the Journey," such as Psalm 130:1: "Out of the depths, I cried to you O Lord" and Psalm 71:20, "You who have shown me many troubles and distresses will revive me again and bring me up again from the depth of the earth."

In what ways is your grief journey like climbing out of a deep crevice or abyss? Ask God to give you the courage to keep climbing.

Read Psalm 130 and make it your own prayer for today. Feel the longing for God's help and for His love that is expressed by the psalmist and make it an expression of your own heart - a request for strength to get out of your canyon.

_____

_____

_____

_____

_____

_____

_____

_____

_____

_____

_____

_____

_____

_____

_____

_____

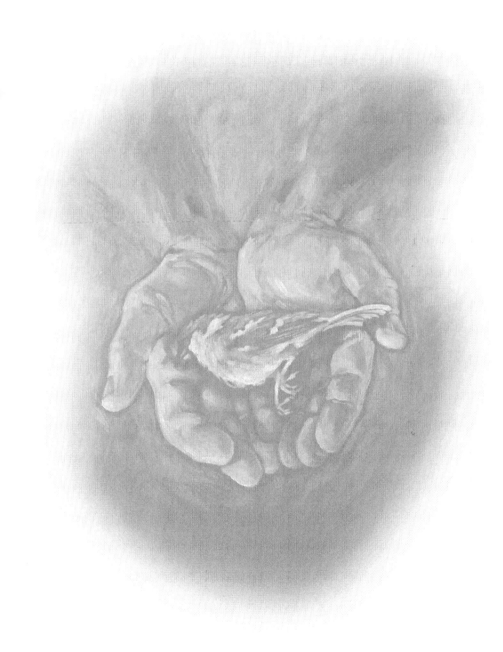

I Thought God Was Good!

I would have despaired unless I had believed that
I would see the goodness of the Lord in the land of the living.
Psalm 27:13

I have heard it said that every griever becomes a theologian. This is because so often God did not act in a way we expected, prayed or hoped He would. He disappointed us. So, we become theologians, trying to understand where we went wrong in our faith or our understanding of God.

A few months before Josiah died I was sitting in a Sunday School class and the topic for discussion was the goodness of God. At one point the teacher said, "One of your greatest tests of faith will be: when everything looks bad, will you continue to believe that God is good?"

I struggled with this thought after his death. I knew that, as it says in Proverbs, "Man is born for trouble as sparks fly upward." I remembered that Jesus said, "In the world you will have tribulation." But I felt – as a child of a loving Father - surely He would have prevented something like *this* from happening.

I knew that God didn't "do this to me." But I still thought "How could You do this to me? And if You didn't do it, how could You let the devil do it to me? I know it was Josiah's decision (a bad decision at that), but couldn't You have prevented it?" I knew He could have and chose not to. That's what kept me awake at night!

I knew it was going to take awhile to sort this out. The God who allowed my son to die is the same God who is now holding me together. How can this be? How can I function with this conflict? I questioned His goodness, but I desperately wanted to experience His goodness. I needed *something* good in my life.

Then I remembered the Sunday School class from a few months prior. Did I really believe in the goodness of God? If one of the two of us was wrong, I was sure it had to be me.

I made a conscious choice to believe that all God does is good. I finally told Him "God, I don't see anything good right now. Life doesn't look good. I don't feel good. What happened to Josiah is not good. But I choose to believe *You are good* despite what I see and feel. And if my view of what You are doing is not good, I choose to believe that the problem is on my end. You are always good. Help me see your goodness today." I found that He is an amazing Redeemer who turns bad into good.

Heavenly Hope

I said to the Lord, "You are my Lord; I have no good besides You."
Psalm 16:2

Do you have enough faith to believe that God is good, in spite of what happened? Are you willing to tell the Lord that you choose to trust that He has good in mind for you and your family? He will show you the good, if you ask Him.

When Moses was confused and afraid of losing the presence of God, he cried out to God "Show me your glory!" What did God show him? (Exodus 33:18, 19)

_____

_____

_____

_____

_____

_____

_____

_____

Holidays and Significant Events

His sons used to go and hold a feast in the house of each one on his day (his birthday!) and they would send and invite their three sisters to eat and drink with them.
Job 1:4

GriefShare facilitators, counselors and books on grief have so many wonderful, practical ideas for handling the holidays. I will defer to them and share some mom-to-mom ideas.

Our first Christmas AJD we intentionally searched out the most pathetic, rejected tree on the lot and dragged it home. Setting it up in the living room actually brought our first Christmas laugh! We all laughed again when we plugged in the lights and only half of them lit up!

For gifts, I purchased small treasure boxes for each sibling and filled them with pictures and mementos from Josiah life. Many moms light a candle and place it by a picture of their child every Christmas, acknowledging their "presence."

During Thanksgiving we placed three kernels of dried corn on each plate and had everyone share something they learned about God through Josiah's death.

At Halloween we reminisced about how Josiah loved sharing his candy more than eating it. We also talked about him sitting on the Waldo Canyon hiking trail in his "Where's Waldo?" costume after posting a sign 100 feet prior asking, "Where's Waldo?" He was just funny like that!

Valentine's Day brought out the heart-shaped biscuits that he loved. Of course, topped with pink frosting!

Josiah loved birthdays, especially his own! He had a way of stretching his birthday into several days with numerous celebrations. One day, about three months before his birthday I saw him sitting, staring off into space. I asked, "Josiah, what are you thinking about?" He answered, "My birthday." I said, "It's not for a few months." "I know" he replied!

The first few years AJD we acknowledged both his birthday and his departure date with a family meal and a trip to the gravesite to place our heart-shaped rocks and share memories.

After awhile his siblings were not so eager to participate. About three years after his death we invited his brothers and sister to dinner on his birthday. His older brother said, "I'll come if we don't sit at the table and sing 'Happy Birthday' to someone who's not there." It was an honest comment that showed us that while they still loved and remembered him, they were moving forward in their lives.

Over the years, holiday memories have gone from bittersweet to better-sweet. Other memories and the need to officially acknowledge "the dates" and make a family pilgrimage to his grave have become not so crucial.

We still acknowledge these, but now it's usually through texting some memories or emailing a photograph or talking about him on the phone. He will never be far from our thoughts during any family gathering.

I'll be home for Christmas

As I listened to the music
Play the sweet refrain
"I'll be Home For Christmas"
My heart cried out in pain:
"No, you won't, you won't be here!"
Your void is everywhere.
A present unbought, a stocking unfilled,
A laden table, an empty chair...
Friends arrive, the family gathers,
Festive laughter fills the air.
I search the sea of faces
Knowing yours will not be there.
Then in my pain, my dream did fade,
The truth stood out so clear:
We are the visitors here on earth,
And you are home this year!
Home with Jesus, Mom and Gram,
And we are left behind.
So know that I'll be home for Christmas,
If only in my mind.

Lynda Shelhamer

Heavenly Hope

Do this in remembrance of Me. Luke 22:19

Jesus created/instituted the celebration of communion to keep the memory of Him and His life fresh in our hearts. Can you think of a positive way to keep the memory of your child alive in your family's holiday celebrations?

What did Mary do with her memories? (Luke 2:19)

The

Court Room

*Oh that I knew where I could find Him that I might come to His
seat. I would present my case before Him
and fill my mouth with arguments!*
Job 23:3, 4

I have mentioned not comparing our grief and loss with others, but
come on, moms, Job did have it worse! He lost 10 kids, his health, his
business, his house, his reputation and many friends. His not-so-
supportive spouse told him to "curse God and die!" He never got a pre-
view of Job chapters 1 & 2 to know the "why" behind his story like we
do.

The book of Job is not about him losing everything and then getting all
his "stuff" back. Rather it is about Job's views and expectations of God
and how drastically they were altered through his grief journey.

Job asked more than 19 "why" questions. Job 23 is one of my very favorite grief sections. Read it, ladies. He's just like us! It refers to his
lack of energy (verse 2), even to the point of an inability to raise his
hand. Then he describes how, if he could go to court with God, he
would have some very good arguments. They would be so good that
God would take note of them (verse 4-6) and deliver him from his
darkness.

I, too, have such good arguments. Just, strong arguments that make total sense as to why God shouldn't have allowed my son to die. But Job cannot find God, to reason with the Judge. He goes forward, backward, right and left, but he cannot see Him. Desperate, spinning, lost, God is silent. (Been there?)

After all this craziness and human reasoning, I love, love his verdict. Verse 10: "*But* He knows the way I take; when He has tested me I *shall* come forth as gold!" Although Job is not seeing God, he knows that God is seeing him and that the end of his story is going to be good.

In Job 40:4 Job finally puts his hand over his mouth and quits *asking* "why" and *acknowledges* "Who." There are dimensions and prisms of God's character that will never be seen in the fragrant flower fields of life. After all, all sunshine makes a desert!

Job knew, like James, that trials produce endurance and endurance produces character. He understood that God is God and we are not. Simple but profound!

Job 42 was Job's last chapter.
The Lord blessed the latter days of Job more than his beginning.

By the end of his life he had 14,000 sheep, 6,000 camels, 1,000 oxen, 1,000 donkeys, (doesn't really sound like a blessing to me!) but hey - seven sons and three beautiful daughters. He lived 140 years and saw his children and grandchildren for four generations.

So Job died, old and full of days.

We do not know our "last chapter." Envision yourself entering God's Courtroom. State your case to God. He loves honesty and invites us into the courtroom.

Come boldly to the throne of grace that we might obtain mercy and grace to help in the time of need. Hebrews 4:16

Read Job's conclusion. (Job 42:1-6)

_____
_____
_____
_____
_____
_____
_____
_____
_____
_____
_____
_____

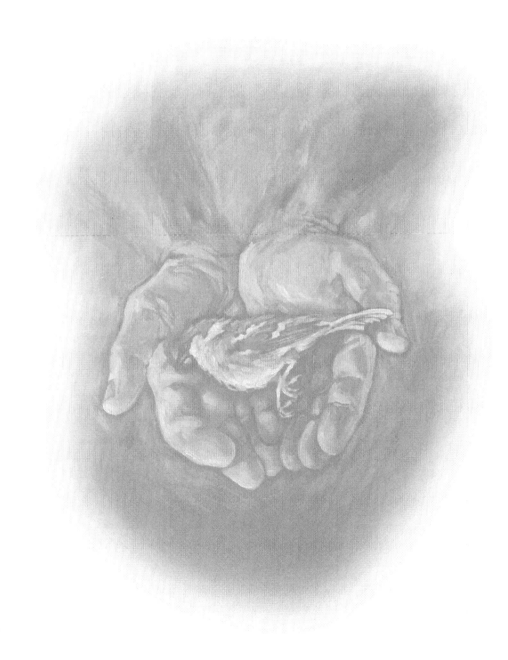

My Secret Garden

*My heart is in anguish within me and the terrors of death have
fallen upon me. Fear and trembling come upon me
and horror has overwhelmed me.*

*I said, "Oh that I had wings like a dove! I would fly away and be at
rest. Behold, I would wander far away. I would lodge in the
wilderness. I would hasten to my place of refuge
from the stormy wind and tempest."*
Psalm 55:4-8

Call me crazy! Call us all crazy but AJD I would entertain silly games in
my head. One such game was playing "make believe" like I was heading
to Josiah's room to wake him up for school. Indulging myself in the old
familiar feeling, I'd walk down the hall saying, "Wake up, Josiah. Wake
up. It's time to get up for school." Of course, opening the door, the
room was dark and empty.

My favorite crazy game was "Hide and Seek." I'd tell myself, "Okay, he's
just hiding and I can't find him." I'd yell as loud as I could, "Come out,
come out wherever you are! I can't *find* you!" Silence.

We all, as kids, loved our secret hiding places. Two of my well-worn
reading books as a child were *Rainbow Gardens* and *The Secret Garden*.
In each the little girl discovers a beautiful secret retreat to where she
can run when she is sad, lonely or scared. People today refer to it as
one's "happy place." But "happy place" ain't happening in grief!

One morning I awoke with the compelling urge to run away and hide. I
jumped in the car and drove down to the Glen Eyrie Castle to hike a
favorite trail and find some heavenly hope and healing.

As I hiked deeper into the woods, storm clouds gathered. "Perfect! Matches my mood." Thunder clapped. "Good, it drowns out the ugly sounds in my head." Lightning flashed. "Fine, take me."

Not wanting to be "here" but not really wanting to die, I began running to my secret place – a waterfall where the mountain's tears overflowed faster and harder than mine. I hid myself under the cleft of a rock and wept with the falls. There, as instructed in Matthew 6:6, I prayed to my Father, Who is in the "secret place." The Great Lover of My Soul whispered, "I will hide you in the shadow of My wings until the storm passes…"

The storm *has* passed. I rarely visit my secret place any more, but I was there last summer. My waterfall of tears is located on the same Glen Eyrie Castle grounds where we held our first *Umbrella Ministries* Conference in Colorado: *Heavenly Hope and Healing for Moms of Loss*. Aren't God's ways amazing? The rainbow of healing had come full circle! There *are* full circle rainbows, you know! Google it!

For in the time of trouble He shall hide me in His pavilion ... in the secret place He shall hide me. He shall set me high upon a rock. Psalm 27:5

Do you have a secret place? Invite God to go there with you and be open to His ministry to you as you linger.

Look up I Kings 19:4-8. Here we find Elijah running a day's journey into the wilderness, sitting under a broom tree, praying that he might die. How does the Angel of The Lord minister to him? What can we glean from his instructions?

_____

_____

_____

_____

_____

_____

_____

_____

_____

_____

_____

_____

_____

_____

_____

_____

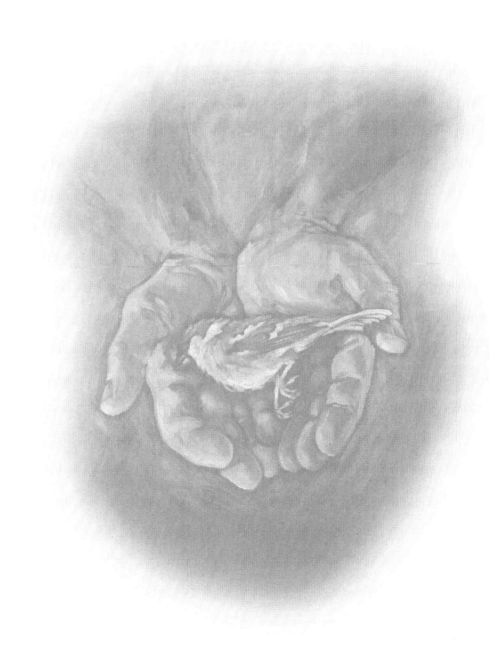

The Anchor And The Hope Rope

This hope we have as an anchor of the soul, both sure and steadfast and which enters the Presence behind the veil.
Hebrews 6:19

I've had two "near drowning" experiences. The first was getting caught in an ocean current, snorkeling off a rocky coast. The second was being overcome by tumultuous waves – swept into a sea of darkness by the strong undertow currents of *grief*. Both sensations were the same: panic, vertigo, frantic kicking – fighting hard while strongly desiring to quit fighting!

David so accurately described this sensation in Psalm 18:4-6: "The cords of death entangled me, the torrents of destruction overwhelmed me ... In my distress I called to the Lord. From His temple He heard my cry." In both situations The Dive Master had His eye on me and came to my rescue.

Are the seaweeds of death seemingly strangling you, pulling you under? Allow The Dive Master to pull you into the life raft.

The life raft itself may be tossed by wind; thrown about in the waves; engulfed by seawater. But it has an anchor that is "sure and steadfast." And look where it is embedded: in the Presence behind the heavenly veil, where Jesus sits on the Mercy Seat! This is our hope, moms.

Romans 5:5: "Hope does not disappoint because the love of God is spread abroad in our hearts." Hang on to the Hope Rope. It is anchored in God's love.

I called out of my distress to the Lord and He answered me. I cried for help from the depth of Sheol; You heard my voice. For You had cast me into the deep, into the heart of the seas, and the current engulfed me. All Your breakers and billows passed over me. So I said, "I have been expelled from Your sight. Nevertheless I will look again toward Your holy temple." Jonah 2:2-4

What can you relate to in Jonah's drowning experience?

Who do we need to 'wake up' in the midst of our storms? (Matthew 8:24-26)

Music's Healing Power

David would take a harp and play it
then Saul would become refreshed and well,
and the distressing spirit would depart from him.
I Samuel 16:23

I grew up in a house surrounded by music. My dad played the saxophone and the clarinet. We all sang in the car on road trips – still do. Guitars were Christmas presents and we all took piano lessons.

Currently, I can only play piano music if there's not more than one sharp or flat - though not well. I can play "Somewhere Over the Rainbow" on my yellow ukulele - though not well.

Two years ago my 95 year-old musician dad passed as I sang to him "What a Friend We Have in Jesus." Though not accomplished in any form of music, I appreciate it all!

Music can touch the soul when nothing else can or will. It will often speak what cannot be expressed.

David's harp soothed Saul's tormented spirit. When my friend Judy's son died, the Carpenters "End of the World" was popular:

> Why does the sun go on shining?
> Why does the sea rush to shore?
> Why do the birds go on singing?
> Why do the stars glow above?
> Why does my heart go on beating?
> Why do these eyes of mine cry?
> Don't they know it's the end of the world?
> It ended when you said "goodbye".

That song forever marked the period when her son died.

"Unchained Melody" (The Righteous Brothers) was popular when Josiah died. I bellowed the words tearfully as I drove, "Oh my love, my darling, I hunger, *hunger* for your touch... yet time moves so slowly; when will you be mine?"

Christian lyrics played me to sleep, such as: "Blessed be the Name ... He gives and takes away; My heart will choose to say, Lord, blessed be Your name ..." It has been said that when pain penetrates, music resonates! God created this melody method of healing and thus the Psalms.

I wrote lullabies for each of my babies. Little did I know how prophetic Josiah's would prove to be. A few of the lines are:

> Josiah, Josiah, the Lord is beside ya.
> Josiah, Josiah, to comfort and guide ya
> And someday Josiah, you'll be His little guy-a.
> And someday Josiah you'll be His boy King!

At our Colorado *Umbrella Ministries* Retreat we enjoyed *Music with Marilyn*. Marilyn shared the composer's own grief story prior to singing each meaningful song. That was so powerful for us. Psalm 33:3 – "Sing to Him a new song." God *will* give you new songs.

Check out her list at: heavenlyhopeandhealing.com/sparrow.

Acts 16:23-25: *The magistrates tore off their clothes, beat them, laid many stripes on them, threw them into the inner prison ... fastened them in stocks ... But about midnight Paul and Silas were praying and singing hymns of praise to God and the prisoners were listening to them.*

Here is an example of Bible characters singing in very dark circumstances. Who were they? And what were their circumstances? Why would they sing at a time like this?

Jesus Himself *sang a hymn* on the night of His betrayal, just as He set His face toward Gethsemane. Matthew 26:30: *And when they had sung a hymn they went out to the Mount of Olives.*

There are three types of song mentioned in Colossians 3:16. What is instructed to be in our hearts as we sing them? Is that possible for you at this time? If not, no guilt. Someday your sparrow will teach you how to sing.

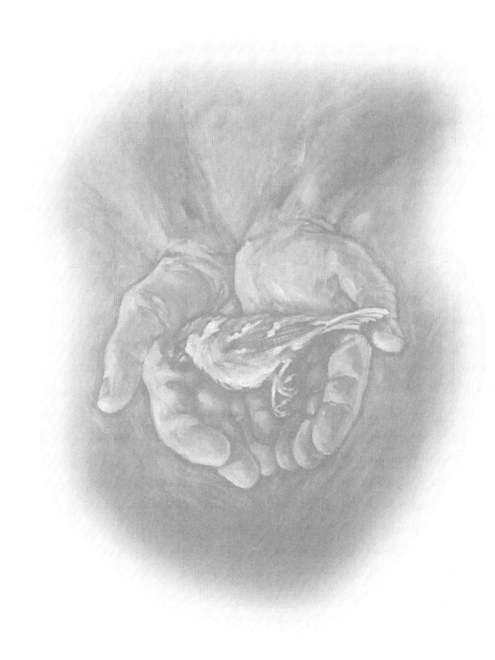

Don't Lose Your Child and Your Spouse

Be kind, compassionate to one another, forgiving each other,
just as in Christ God forgave you.
Ephesians 4:32

Some say the rate of divorce is higher after the death of a child. Others say that this is a myth and really the existing condition of the marriage may be accentuated by the stress upon the relationship.

Our marriage was strong, but we definitely found it harder to connect with each other. Both of us were kicking and treading so hard just to keep our own heads above water – how could we possibly reach out and help the other? *Everything* was drained emotionally so there was nothing left to offer the other.

You've heard the story about the last straw on the camel's back? It felt like *everything* was the last straw. It can become easier and maybe safer to isolate oneself rather than to be constantly irritated or angry.

We both lost the same child, but our individual grieving was very unique and different. Social mores tell men they shouldn't cry. They are the strong ones and the protectors of the family. Also, men are more task-oriented, so they frequently work out their grief through their job.

I learned that just because my husband, John, wasn't crying or talking as much as I was, it didn't mean he was suppressing his grief. Your husband is probably not going to talk, cry or meet your emotional needs as much as you would like him to.

We did sob and hold each other a lot, but I learned to turn to "the Man of Sorrows, acquainted with grief" to meet my deepest needs and emotional hurts.

Regarding sexual intimacy, it was that intimate act that created the child we lost. That act could become a painful reminder of the loss rather than the positive personal moment it should be. It was a subject that required some time and open discussion to move forward to enjoyment again.

Love never fails. I Corinthians 13:8

Just like we have to trust God's love for us even though He may seem absent or aloof for a season, can you trust the fact that your husband's love is there even during the absent and aloof times? Would today be a good time to tell him that?

We can only love one another when we understand how Christ has loved us, John 13:34. In what ways has Christ loved you? List them.

_____

_____

_____

_____

_____

_____

_____

_____

_____

Comparing Wounds

I am afflicted and needy,
my heart is wounded within me.
Psalm 109:22

As a nurse I've done a lot of wound care. Wounds all heal differently. Some quickly; some more slowly. Occasionally wounds lay gaping, open for years – deep, purulent wounds. C.S. Lewis said the death of a beloved is like an amputation, although the same leg is cut again and again.

Moms, this is why we cannot compare our grief. One may lose a thumb, and another a leg. One's wound may appear to be healing more quickly while others appear to be open and festering. All "child wounds" are deep and painful. They require daily attention and care. Amputations require learning how to adapt and function around the loss.

Each one's pain and healing journey is unique. It took lots of conscious effort on my part not to compare my child's death with another. I am sure others find the same challenge.

The real challenge is when someone who is whole and wound-free comes dancing into your life. Resentment, self-pity and jealousy naturally surface—especially if they come dancing in with their kids and family phone-photos of special occasions and celebrations.

It is not their fault that they don't have wounds, and we don't know the end of their story. They in turn have no idea how painful it is for us with festering wounds to see them dancing and seemingly flaunting their cute pictures and stories.

Once more I had to turn to "The Man of Sorrows Who *is acquainted* with grief" for understanding and sympathy.

The other challenge we face is relating to others who have experienced what we might consider a *lesser* loss. They try to demonstrate they know what we're going through as they seek to console us and we're thinking, "They have no idea what my wound is like." What has helped me is to realize that whether they have a cut or a slash or an amputation, if they are experiencing more pain than they have ever experienced before, it is not all that different than my pain.

He bruises but He binds up the wounds and His hands make whole. Job 5:1

He heals the broken hearted and binds up their wounds. Psalm 147:3

What are some ways in which God is giving attention to your wound? What has He done to help "bind it?"

I just love these verses; they are God's promises to me when I'm at the end of my rope! (Isaiah 42:3; Psalm 34:18)

_____

_____

_____

_____

_____

_____

_____

_____

_____

_____

_____

Missing Puzzle Pieces

The secret things belong to the Lord our God,
but the things revealed belong to us.
Deuteronomy 29:29

We all have a few strange friends who like to do puzzles. Large, complicated 5,000 piece puzzles. The more challenging, the better. Not me! Give me a 100-piece puzzle and that only during the holidays!

I do, in fact, envy anyone who has time in our busy world to sit at a quiet table and search for a puzzle piece. I'll stand there looking at the pile of pieces for twenty minutes and only find one piece.

In grief we have been handed a box of puzzling puzzle pieces. Many pieces seemingly are missing. Others just don't appear to fit together at all. We sit at the table, in our minds trying to assemble the un-assemble-able, desperately searching for the missing pieces.

Confused, I wanted God to hand over all the pieces so that I could fit them into a picture that made sense. In retrospect, I see God's wisdom in not giving me all the pieces at once. I know now that there are pieces I couldn't have handled. You may stand staring at your puzzle for five years and find only one piece.

I found that, like the brother who mischievously hides the key puzzle pieces, I too, hid pieces. These secret puzzle pieces I kept hidden for years deep in my pocket. It took time and trust in the love of God before I could pull them out and place them on the table.

The back of our puzzles may look like gray cardboard with lots of empty areas. Don't drive yourself crazy looking for that one missing piece.

The Puzzle Designer has them in His pocket and may hand them to you when you least expect it. For me it was several years down the road.

The Bible promises that in heaven we will be handed the missing last piece. "There is nothing concealed that will not be revealed or hidden that will not be known." Matthew 10:26

Heavenly Hope

It is the glory of God to conceal a matter, but the glory of kings is to search out a matter. Proverbs 25:2

The secret things belong to the Lord our God, but the things revealed belong to us and to our sons forever. Deuteronomy 29:29

What puzzle piece would you like to be handed today?

Is your focus on the missing puzzle pieces or on the Puzzle Designer?

What can you discover about The Puzzle Maker's ways? (Romans 11:33; Isaiah 55:8, 9)

_____

_____

_____

_____

_____

_____

_____

Beam Me Up, Scotty

Oh that I had wings like a dove.
I would fly away and be at rest.
Psalm 55:6

In my early grieving process I just wanted to be transported ahead two years. I imagined by that time the pain would be less. I wanted Scotty in Star Trek to beam me up and instantly remove me from my nightmare. Can anyone relate?

I often hear that grieving moms don't want to die; they just don't want to *be here*. Sometimes we do want to die and if you're serious about that and have a plan, please let someone know today.

I used to play "Want to go on a lion hunt?" with my toddlers. As we approached the gate, swamp and lake, we would say, "Can't go under it, can't go around it, have to go through it." Slosh, Slosh, Slog, Slog.

As much as we want to run or hide from the big black cloud of grief, the only choice we have is to go through it. Isaiah 43:2 states, "When you pass *through* the waters I will be with you and *through* the rivers; they will not overflow you. When you walk *through* the fire you will not be scorched, nor will the flames burn you, for I am the Lord, your God."

The book of Hebrews states that Jesus, "For the joy set before Him endured the cross, despising the shame." The *Hall of Faith* in Hebrews 11 cites many terrible things saints went through in order to receive their reward or what was promised them.

There is joy and blessing ahead, but as in our lion hunt game, we will have to slog through the muddy, damp, dark, swamp to get there.

Our God Whom we serve is able to deliver us from the burning fiery furnace, but, if not, let it be known we will not serve your gods...
Daniel 3: 17, 18

Shadrach, Meshach and Abednego were being forced to step into a fiery furnace seven times hotter than what would kill a normal person. What was their determined declaration prior to entry?

What is your determination regarding the fire you are walking through?

The same Person who stood with them in their fiery furnace is standing with you. Who is it? (Daniel 3:25)

What was on the other side of their "Fiery Furnace" experience?
(Daniel 3:27-3)

_____

_____

_____

_____

_____

_____

_____

_____

_____

_____

_____

_____

_____

_____

The Refiner's Fire

He knows the way I take and
when He has tried me I shall come forth as gold.
Job 23:10

Moms, God did not allow our children to die to *punish* us. But He will use their death to *purify* us!

Malachi 3:2, 3 portrays God sitting at the smelter, skillfully purifying His beloved children as silver and gold. The fire in a smelter is different from other fires. Unlike Colorado's forest fires that jump and devour at random, or like an incinerator that destroys its entire contents, God's fire has a purpose and that purpose is not to incinerate us or leave us burnt and bare.

The Refiner, Himself, is a craftsman. He knows the exact temperature (2,000 degrees!) and duration of time it will require to make pure gold – not 10- karat, or 14-karat, but 24-karat pure gold.

I imagine the gold, hot and extremely uncomfortable, screaming, "Stop, enough is enough! I'll just be 10-karat. Or, how about just let me be fool's gold?" As the gold is heated and purified, the slag or dross rises to the top and is discarded.

I don't like either of those words. Slag looks like slug and dross like gross. However, I am sure I have plenty of both in my life. Beauty doesn't come easy. God is purifying for Himself a beautiful bride, but – and read this out loud – He is not punishing His bride! He loves His bride.

Heavenly Hope

In I Peter 4:12, 13, God tells us not to be surprised (yeah, right ...) at the fiery ordeal, *but to the degree (2,000° in fact) you share in the sufferings, keep on rejoicing.*

How are you sharing in the suffering of Christ in your trial?

Peter ends this chapter with: *Therefore those also who suffer according to the will of God shall entrust their souls to a faithful Creator.*

Would you consider telling God, even right now, how difficult it is to trust Him, but that *you do* trust him?

The adjective James uses to describe "trials" in James 1:2 is "various" or "varied." In the Greek it actually means trials of different colors! What color would you describe your trial?

_____

_____

_____

_____

_____

_____

_____

_____

_____

_____

_____

_____

_____

_____

Where Was God When Josiah Died?

And Lo, I am with you even until the end of the world.
Matthew 28:20

As a hospice nurse, I was at Velma's bedside the afternoon she died. I noticed she kept staring up into the corner of the room with a big smile on her face. Finally I asked her, "Velma, what do you see?" She said, "I see angels." I asked, "What are they doing?" Staring into the corner again she replied, "Having a party!" "For whom, Velma?" "For *me!*" Shortly after this she passed.

I have had the privilege of being with many people on their deathbed. Believe me; I have the intel on this one. There is a lot of activity in heaven when a human dies. Often patients describe angels, seeing Jesus or loved ones who have passed before them.

One of my favorite stories in the Bible is in Acts 7:55, 56, where we find Stephen being dragged by an angry mob to his death by stoning. The heavens open and Stephen sees Jesus standing at the right hand of God. Normally Jesus is portrayed as sitting at the right hand, but as Stephen is dying from what would be a very painful death, Jesus is *standing*, and all heaven is active! Stephen's face is shining like an angel.

I Corinthians 15:55, 56 refers to the *"sting* of death" – the painful part – being taken away for the Christ-followers. I've watched many peaceful faces on dying saints that should have been painful faces, as they take their last breath.

Where was God? He was in the same place He was when His own Son was dying: watching, weeping, then tearing the veil open, making an entrance to heaven for all eternity!

My son wrote about his vision as he was dying. I have saved it for you all as a special gift at the end of this journal – no peeking!

This child is appointed for the fall and the rise of many in Israel and for a sign to be opposed, and a sword will pierce even your own soul ...
Luke 2:34, 35

Simeon the prophet handed Mary this horrible prophecy about her baby. Why would God allow Mary to look on her Son's brutally beaten body hanging on the cross and feel her soul pierced as the soldier pierced His side? If you were with your child when he/she died, can you see that your presence there was God's kindness toward your child?

What was Mary's response to the prophecies she received?
(Luke 1:46-55)

_____

_____

_____

_____

_____

_____

_____

_____

Expectations of Self

My soul, wait only upon God,
for my expectation is from Him.
Psalm 62:5

A wise friend once counseled me, "Lower your expectations and you won't be disappointed!"

As US citizens, we are born into a country of high expectations. Our own Constitution tells us we have "the right to life, liberty and the pursuit of happiness."

Yet C.S. Lewis wrote, "If you think of this world as a place intended for our happiness you will find it quite intolerable. Think of it instead as a place of training and it's not so bad!"

I once housed a Chernobyl victim from Romania. In a conversation she shared, "What amazes me about you Americans is you are surprised by suffering. We in Romania accept it as a daily part of our lives."

Reluctantly, I lowered my expectations of myself, my time, my energy and I experienced a great relief. I didn't send a thank you note for every dish of lasagna and didn't respond to every card and phone call. I gave up "being better" by such – and – such date.

I just curled up in my fetal position under the quilt and hung on to hope. Not the kind of hope that "hopes to get something" but hope in the character of God, that He is indeed a loving Father Who has my family's best – and my best interest in mind. Job 13:15: *"Though He slay me, yet I will hope in Him."*

Heavenly Hope

Now hope does not disappoint because the LOVE of God has been poured out in our hearts by the Holy Spirit Who has been given to us. Romans 5:5

Why does hope not disappoint? Check yourself: are your expectations of yourself realistic?

Where did David, who lost two children, find his hope? (Psalm 39:7; Psalm 71)

_____

_____

_____

_____

_____

_____

_____

_____

_____

_____

_____

_____

_____

_____

_____

_____

_____

_____

Expectations of Others

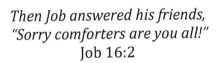

Then Job answered his friends,
"Sorry comforters are you all!"
Job 16:2

Family, friends and fellow employees are going to say stupid things! Practice not taking it to heart. And believe me it does take practice; even Job found his friends to be sorry comforters!

Shortly after Josiah's death I was doing homecare for an elderly patient who had heard my story. Trying to comfort me she said, "Think of all the money you'll save on graduation, college and weddings."

I know all of you have similar stories. There's always the "I know how you feel" stories that end with "I lost a dog" or a grandmother. I learned to make a conscious effort to look past people's words to their intention. This sweet old lady was groping for something to ease my pain and this was all she could think of!

Personally, prior to losing a child, I had no idea of how painful the loss of a child could be and neither do those around you. So live and give grace.

I was fully aware after my son died of how poorly I had reached out to others in their loss and my unrealistic expectations of them. This is why you want to find and hang with moms who have had similar experiences; moms whose eyes you can look into and intuitively feel: "What? You too? I thought I was the only one!"

And the Lord restored Job's losses when he prayed for his friends.
Job 42:10

Job found restoration when he did what?

My friends are my scoffers. Job 16:20

Indeed Job's friends made his suffering more difficult. They were more interested in being right than being good friends. Recognize that your friends may not know how to help you or minister to you. They may have no idea how deep your pain goes. Consider searching out a support group with others who have experienced loss.

Do you sense that people and friends are treating you differently? (Psalm 38:10, 11; Psalm 55:12-14)

_____

_____

_____

_____

_____

_____

_____

_____

_____

_____

_____

 *Memories*

The righteous will be remembered forever.
Psalm 112:6

In the song, "Memories" the lines read, "Memories may be beautiful, and yet, what's too painful to remember, we simply choose to forget." If only choosing to forget *was easy!* But memories are like the sky, spread over everywhere: an empty chair, a favorite food or restaurant, an unplayed game, a favorite park.

For me, early on, every happy memory was sad and brought tears. I wanted to remember while desperately wanting to forget. I did not want the memory of my son's death to eclipse all the beautiful moments of his life. Yet for a while it was all I could think of regarding my son. Holidays were especially poignant with reminders: unpurchased presents, a vacant place at the table, an empty stocking on the fireplace.

Dr. Seuss said: "Don't cry because it's over, smile because it happened."

Taking Dr. Seuss' advice, I began putting together a photo album of Josiah's life. A friend kindly offered to sit with me and graciously listened as I shared memories and held each picture, laughing and crying.

Another mom I know took it on herself to gather and record 100 memories of her child. Besides creating a beautiful document, she found it therapeutic for herself, her husband, the siblings and friends to be given permission to speak about the unspeakable.

Your memories will someday go from bittersweet to better-sweet and you will smile again!

Heavenly Hope

The Lord gave attention and heard it, so a Book of Remembrance was written before Him for those who fear the Lord and who meditate on His name. Malachi 3:16

For whom does God write His book of remembrance? What are you doing to help preserve (but not enshrine) the memory of your child? In years to come you will find it helpful to revisit these positive memories.

What does Jeremiah remember when his hope is gone?
(Lamentations 3:18-25)

_____

_____

_____

_____

_____

_____

_____

_____

_____

_____

_____

_____

_____

_____

_____

_____

The Shadow of Death Valley

*Even though I walk through the Valley of the Shadow of Death
I will fear no evil, for You are with me.*
Psalm 23:4

The dark valley you are walking through may not feel like a shadow. Yet David, who lost two children, called this *the valley of the shadow of death*. Shadows can be big, dark and scary but they can't physically hurt you.

Satan will cast many big scary shadows on your path in the form of imaginations, accusations, lies and thoughts that we don't know to be true.

My husband and I were biking through a canyon in Moab, Utah, when suddenly a huge dark form came careening toward us. Instinctively I searched for a place to take cover. Soon the source revealed itself: a small hawk reflecting its shadow on the narrow canyon wall, but I swear the shadow was at least twenty feet long!

C. S. Lewis describes this planet we live on as "the Shadow Lands," just a reflection of reality.

Become an expert at taking these shadows and aligning them with the *True North* compass of God's word. This practice has kept me from becoming totally lost in *The Valley of Grief*.

Climbing mountains in Colorado, I have seen that the views are terrific above timberline, but nothing grows at that altitude. Looking down on the *valleys* I notice it is there that verdant, lush growth is taking place! Keep in mind, moms, it takes two mountains to form a valley.

Take courage, there is a mountain-top experience ahead. Experience the green growth in *your valley*.

Heavenly Hope

Casting down imaginations and every high thing that exalts itself against the knowledge of God and bring into captivity every thought to the obedience of Christ. II Corinthians 10:5

What does God tell us to do with our imaginations?

Behold, You desire truth in the innermost being; and in the hidden part You will make me know wisdom. Psalm 51:6

Write down the imaginations and fears that haunt you. Next to each imagination or fear write what you know to be true, the True North.

What other Shadows are referred to in the Bible? (Psalms 17:8; Psalms 91:1,2)

_____

_____

_____

_____

_____

_____

_____

_____

_____

_____

_____

_____

_____

Your Wailing Wall

Clothe yourself with sackcloth, lament and wail.
Jeremiah 4:8

Throughout history, most religions and cultures have traditions involving mourning the dead. Some seem quite bizarre, like making a life-sized clay image of the deceased and keeping it in the house.

Traditions of wearing black date back to Roman times and still exist in many cultures.

Hindus place a lit oil lamp in the house for three days; they then are required to end mourning after 13 days. Islam mourns four lunar months and ten days, wearing no jewelry or decorative clothing. Shrieking and wailing are not permitted, nor the tearing of clothes.

The Jewish mourning period is called "Shiva" and occurs for seven days following the death. Mirrors are covered. The family sits on uncomfortable chairs wearing a mangled black ribbon and slippers. A candle is lit for seven days and again yearly on the anniversary date.

During the Victorian Era jewelry was sometimes made from the deceased one's hair, symbolic flowers were engraved on the tomb and black veils were often worn.

The Wailing Wall in Jerusalem is a small limestone section of the Western Wall, which for decades has been a gathering place for Jews to mourn.

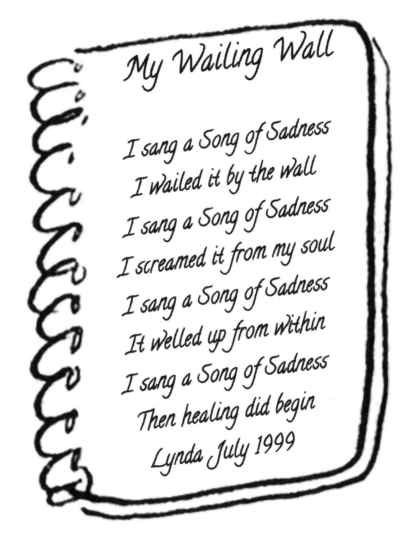

My Wailing Wall

I sang a Song of Sadness
I wailed it by the wall
I sang a Song of Sadness
I screamed it from my soul
I sang a Song of Sadness
It welled up from within
I sang a Song of Sadness
Then healing did begin

Lynda July 1999

For me, in less than a week the funeral was over and I was left standing like a deer in the headlights, not knowing what to do next. No wailing wall to run to or black veil to wear over my sad face. No course in Grieving 101.

I began establishing my own rituals. Screaming Rock: an isolated spot near Red Rocks Canyon. (Come to Colorado; it's a hike but I'll take you there and we can scream together.) Art Therapy with a neighbor, weekly splattering red and black paint together to express our anger and grief.

The Survivor Show was popular and a fellow mom and I decided we definitely qualified as "survivors." Together we bought wash-off "Survivor" tattoos and secretly wore them.

God instructed the Israelites to set up memorials. Today I collect heart-shaped rocks and place them on Josiah's grave. I wear a picture locket around my neck. Other moms have had quilts or teddy bears made from their kid's garments, or T shirts made with their kid's pictures on them – all nice modern day memorials.

Recently I have discovered *GriefShare* (www.GriefShare.org) and *Umbrella Ministries* (www.UmbrellaMinistries.com) to be a very helpful next step after the funeral. Had I discovered them earlier I may not have had to drag my tattooed arm to Red Rock Canyon to scream.

Jesus wept. So the Jews were saying 'See how He loved him!'
John 11:35, 36

We weep even though we have hope for our child's resurrection. Does it help you to know that Jesus wept even though He knew that Lazarus would be resurrected?

What was "Rachel" weeping for and why? (Matthew 2:18)

The Garden of Gethsemane was Jesus' wailing wall. What are words the Scripture uses to describe His sorrow? (Mark 14:33-36)

_____

_____

_____

_____

_____

_____

_____

_____

_____

_____

_____

_____

_____

_____

_____

_____

_____

Jesus Loves Me, This I Know

I have loved you with an everlasting love.
Therefore I have drawn you with lovingkindness.
Jeremiah 31:3

Growing up in Sunday School I loved singing this song, standing with my chin high in the air bellowing, "Yes, Jesus loves me!" ... Then Josiah died.

I felt like I had lost everything, including a good part of my perfectly packed theology. But I knew, *knew*, I could not lose the truth that Jesus loves me. I desperately clung to this truth singing softly, with tears streaming down, hoping to wash away any doubt.

Guess what, moms, now I not only sing, "Jesus loves me this I know," but "Jesus knows me, this I love."

Everything God has allowed to happen in my life is on the radar of a loving God. Every attack of Satan will be redeemed by my loving Father – not always prevented, but redeemed. Every human fault I may have had in my child's death ... redeemed.

If you're reading this in your early entrance into this dark tunnel, this truth may be hard to grasp. Trust me; the light at the end of the tunnel is not a train. It is God's love. Trust the heartbeat of your Father's love for you.

About four months into grief my husband prayed, "God, I know you love me. You have told me so in Your Word and I believe it is true. But, honestly, I don't see it and I don't feel it. Maybe you could show me how You have been loving me."

Right away, God began flooding him with memories of how so many friends, both believers and those who were not believers, had expressed God's love through their own love and their acts of kindness.

He was so humbled by God's response that he ended up writing to all of them, thanking them for being used by God to express His love to our family.

For this is love, not that we loved God, but that He loved us.
I John 4:10

The emotion of grief is so powerful it may have overshadowed your sense of God's love for you. You may find that you need to affirm your belief in God's love for you.

Ask Him to show you how He has been loving you. You may find it helpful to write down all the acts of love and kindness God has shown to you through others.

What or who can separate you from the Love of God? (Romans 8:38, 39; Jude 1:20, 21)

_____

_____

_____

_____

_____

_____

_____

_____

_____

_____

Why Me? Why My Child?

He causes the rain to fall on the just and on the unjust.
Matthew 5:45

You may have heard it said: "The real question is not 'why me' but 'why not me?'" Would you want it to be someone else? (Of course we would, but we wouldn't say it!)

Twice I've been evacuated for wildfires in Colorado. Everyone's eye is on the wind and which way it is going to steer the ravenous flames: my neighborhood or theirs?

I remember a huge sense of relief, mixed with guilt, when it roared towards another neighborhood. God is God and we are not. Job, after losing all of his children said, "Should I accept good from the hand of the Lord and not evil?" (Job 2:10)

The Master Weaver is weaving a much more intricate design than we can see from our tangled side of the tapestry. Isaiah 57:1, 2 tells us that sometimes the righteous die young to save them from the evil to come. Footnotes explain that this is actually a prophecy about King Josiah's death. King Josiah was one of the godliest kings of Israel, yet he was killed at a relatively young age.

His tapestry we do get to see. He was spared seeing two of his sons "do evil in the sight of the Lord, despising His word," and leading his beloved country into captivity. He was spared witnessing his son, Zedekiah's eyes being gouged out after watching his children murdered!

From what horrible things may our merciful God have possibly spared our children?

Heavenly Hope

The righteous perish and no one understands that the righteous are taken away to be spared from evil. He enters into peace and rests in his bed. Isaiah 57:1, 2

Where does the righteous man, who was spared from evil, go? Are you able to accept this?

What does Job say about our acceptance of evil? (Job 2:10)

What was the big WHY that Jesus asked on the cross? (Mark 15:34)

_____

_____

_____

_____

_____

_____

_____

_____

_____

_____

_____

_____

_____

_____

Embracing
a New Normal

See, I am doing a new thing!
Now it springs up; do you not perceive it?
I am making a way in the wilderness
and streams in the wasteland.
Isaiah 43:19

Your circumstances may have shaped who you are but *you* are responsible for who you become. So many "new things" have come into my life through Josiah's death – streams in the wasteland, artesian wells springing up – new friendships, new activities and new hobbies.

My neighbor, Mary Lee, whom I knew only through carpooling, lost her beautiful 12-year-old daughter, Breanna, shortly after Josiah died. Though neither of us had ever even drawn a decent stick figure, we began doing what we called "art therapy" together.

Meeting at my house we would splatter red and black paint together until we laughed and cried. Through this simple shared activity God began to weave our souls together. Today, 18 years later, we are still BFF's.

Chris, to whom I was introduced because we both lost our kids (she lost both of her children), is another BFF. Daily we hike 3-4 miles finding nurturing in nature and each other. We're going on our fourth year together.

I never gardened BJD. Now planting and watching green things <u>live</u> and grow is my new happy hobby. It is the antithesis to death!

Dr. Paul Tripp, in the *GriefShare* video, shares a tremendous insight that "God will take us where we don't want to go, to produce in us things that we could not achieve on our own."

By attending *GriefShare, Umbrella* retreats, *Compassionate Friends* etc. you will find yourself inducted into a new circle of friends. We all say it's a club we never wanted to join but it is a club where we are with people who understand us in a way most old friends never will.

Be open to these new friendships and opportunities and God will take it from there.

Old things have passed away, new things have come. II Corinthians 5:17

What is God busy doing in your life?

Life will never be the same as it was. Can you believe that life being different does not mean that life will be worse?

How do we comfort each other? (II Corinthians 1:4)

Consider inviting one of your new friends for coffee.

_____

_____

_____

_____

_____

_____

_____

_____

_____

_____

Lonely and Abandoned

I will not abandon you as orphans.
I will come to you.
John 14:18

I wanted to be alone but I hated feeling so lonely! Looking back in my grief journal I had written: "I feel so empty, so alone, so abandoned."

I had *empty arms*, missing the touch and smell of my son. Even though I was surrounded by so many people at work, I wanted to quit my job and have more alone time.

Abandoned! God felt aloof. My husband and kids were dealing in their own way with their grief. Mostly I felt abandoned by Josiah. "How could you leave, my love? Josiah, Josiah, why have you forsaken me?"

Jesus promised: "I will never leave you nor forsake you" (Hebrews 13:5). I look out my window and understand that because my beautiful bluebirds are gone and their houses deserted doesn't mean they're not "out there" existing. Existing, with an anticipation to return. Maybe, just maybe, that's how God feels about me as I shiver in my cold, dark winter.

That spring I watched the bluebirds return to their abandoned house after a very cold winter. At first I felt wonderment that they could return so casually to an area that had been so devastated and abandoned.

Spring was the first time I felt a sprout of hope in my heart. The earth awoke and surrounded me with its newness and renewal. The bluebirds returned.

Then I felt, deep inside me, a small quiver of hope. Maybe if they could return and live again in their abandoned house and create life and sing again, maybe I could too!

At the Easter service, I blended my voice with my son's in heaven and worshiped the Living King, feeling closeness with Josiah knowing that we were both bowing before the same throne.

Heavenly Hope

My beloved responded and said to me: "Arise, my darling, my beautiful one and come along, for behold, the winter is past ... the flowers have already appeared in the land ... the voice of the turtledove has been heard in the land ... the vines in blossom have given forth their fragrance. Arise, my darling, my beautiful and come along!"
Song of Solomon 2:10-13

Can you imagine a spring following your winter?

Bask in the love that The Rose of Sharon / The Lily of the Valley has for you this morning. (Song of Solomon 2)

_____

_____

_____

_____

_____

_____

_____

_____

_____

_____

_____

My Broken Shell Collection

The sacrifices of God are a broken spirit;
A broken and contrite heart,
O God, You will not despise.
Psalm 51:17

Come with me this morning on an early morning beach walk. The off-shore winds whip our hair and jackets and bring the smell and taste of salty air. We inhale deeply. Salt is known to cleanse wounds.

The cacophony of morning sounds greets us – seagulls squawk searching the water for breakfast. Rhythmic waves dance with the shoreline, kissing our bare toes. The endless horizon is gone from our view ... like our children.

Look! The pink sun is rising now, lighting up the waters. I look at you and your face is reflecting its pink glow. We smile and enjoy a deep sigh of temporary peace.

Suddenly we're caught off guard in our ocean oasis by a large crashing wave, knocking us to our knees. Struggling, we get up only to be knocked down by the bigger wave behind it. So much like grief! However, I am beginning to notice a pattern here: the largest, most threatening waves are laying the most beautiful of gifts on the sandy shores!

We head inland for a dry towel, a hot cup of latte and conversation.

I used to search for the perfect *unbroken* shells and sand dollars in the wake of a storm.

Now I'm drawn to the *broken* ones.

I tenderly pick one up. Who or what broke this shell? What did it look like in its wholeness? Did it once live among bright red coral, swarming colored fish and waving sea grass? Did it produce a life that still exists, or was its life swallowed by predators, like mine was?

I leave the perfect shells for someone whose life has the illusion of being a bit more perfect. Like mine used to be!

The sun is fully up and I hold my *broken* shell to its light. It glimmers with a pearlized, patterned, pink pastel. The light begins to glow through, reminding me of the glow I noticed on your face this morning.

Broken shells. We're all broken shells. I love my Broken Shells!

Heavenly Hope

2 Corinthians 4:6: *"For God Who said 'Light shall shine out of darkness' is the One Who has shone in our hearts to give the light of the knowledge of the glory of God in the face of Christ."*

Think about your broken shell. Hold it up to the light of the Son this morning. What do you see?

What becomes visible when exposed to the light? (Ephesians 5:13; Isaiah 45:7; Isaiah 50:10; Isaiah 58:8)

_____

_____

_____

_____

_____

_____

_____

_____

_____

_____

Is My Child In Heaven?

Suffer the little children to come unto me
for such is the kingdom of heaven.
Matthew 19:14

Son of my Soul where did you go? Blessed is the mom who can say, "I didn't lose my child. I know exactly where he/she is – heaven!" However, I've talked to enough moms to know that not all moms have this assurance.

One thing we do know is that God's love and salvation reach to the uttermost and the *guttermost*. He is not willing that any should perish but that all come to the knowledge of Him (II Peter 3:9).

Rev. E.V. Hill explains that it's not like God is in His lifeboat, batting people away with a two-by-four saying, "You're not good enough." No, He's so anxious to save, He's grabbing them every way He can, by the arm, by the leg, by the hair trying to get them into His boat.

Salvation is not based on how good or bad a person has been, but whether that person's faith for salvation has been placed in the cross of Jesus Christ. I for one do not want to be the judge deciding how much faith is enough to save. The wayward thief crucified with Christ merely said, "Jesus, remember me ..." The thief was told just before his dying breath, "Today you will be with Me in paradise." Luke 23:42, 43

As a hospice nurse and based on my own son's dying note (which I will share with you at the end), I can tell you that we have no idea how God was manifesting Himself to our child at his or her dying moment.

Trust that God is a good, kind, loving, forgiving Father who has given His Son for us. He was not surprised or caught off guard by your child's death.

The Lord is ... patient toward you, not wishing for any to perish but for all to come to repentance. II Peter 3:9

Can you trust His love and have faith that He spoke to your child before and during his/her final moments? Can you trust that what He did in and for your child was filled with goodness, kindness and infinite love and forgiveness?

What is God's promise to us during and at the *end* of our life? (Matthew 28:20)

Journal your own assurance of salvation (John 3:16).

_____

_____

_____

_____

_____

_____

_____

_____

_____

_____

_____

_____

_____

_____

_____

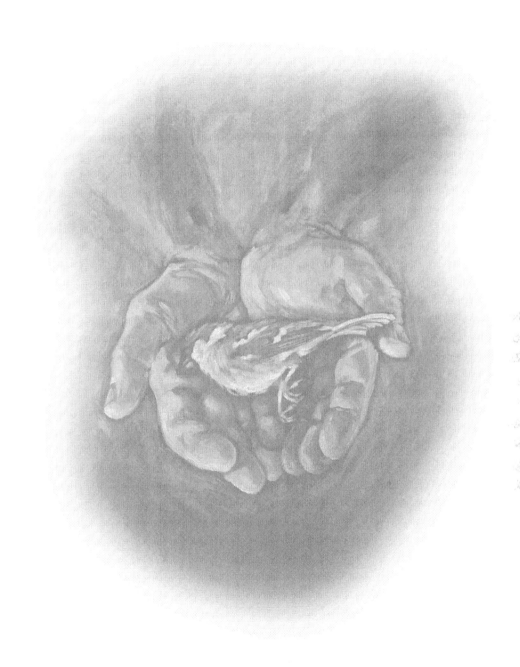

Really? An Attitude of Gratitude?

To You I shall offer a sacrifice of thanksgiving
and call upon the Name of the Lord.
Psalm 116:17

Sometimes the sacrifice of thanksgiving is just that, a sacrifice! Sacrifices are costly. King David said, "I will not offer a sacrifice that costs me nothing."

St. John of Avila said, "One act of thanksgiving when things go wrong is worth one thousand thanks when things are agreeable."

In her book, *One Thousand Gifts*, Ann Voskamp describes how, after crying "blood tears," cutting on herself and struggling with depression, she challenged herself to write down 1000 things for which she was thankful. This became her healing. I took this challenge and to this day my husband and I daily list things for which we are thankful.

Jesus, on His darkest night, the night of His betrayal, "took the cup and *gave thanks.*" After singing a song, He set His face toward the torture of the cross (Matthew 26:27-30). If He can do it, ladies, we can too.

The act of offering thanks is a choice. In the wake of death, it is often a difficult choice – which makes it even that much more a costly sacrifice. In the book of Psalms there are more Psalms of lament than any other type of Psalm. Nearly every one of these begins with a lament or complaint and ends with thanksgiving.

 Heavenly Hope

Do not be anxious about anything, but in every situation, by prayer and petition, with thanksgiving, present your requests to God and the Peace of God will guard your heart and mind in Christ Jesus. Philippians 4:6

What can be the result of praying with thanksgiving? Are you able to look around you and identify things to thank God for?

One of my favorite stories in the Bible is found in II Chronicles, chapter 20. A great army was coming at Jehoshaphat from every side. Do you feel that way? Read his crazy battle plan and its results in II Chronicles 20:21, 22.

_____

_____

_____

_____

_____

_____

_____

_____

_____

_____

_____

_____

_____

_____

_____

 *My Broken Heart*

The Lord is near to the broken hearted
and saves those who are crushed in spirit.
Psalm 34:18

My bare feet track footprints in the wet sand as I scour the beach in Morro Bay for a heart-shaped rock or shell. My search was about to be filed in my "efforts in futility" category when ... bam ... right in front of me was a heart-shaped coral with lots of holes in it, just like my heart. I carefully wrapped it for a suitcase ride back to Colorado to be placed in my "Hi, Mom, From Heaven" collection.

However, the first cold, snowy Colorado winter cracked the coral heart in several places, reflecting *my* heart even more accurately. As I glued it back together with a hot glue gun, the Holy Spirit seemed to say, "With what are you filling the cracks in your broken heart?"

I knew that I had begun overspending, shopping, drinking that second glass of wine, becoming increasingly busy, desperately trying to fill those cracks and empty holes. The cracks are going to be filled with something, so be aware of how they are being filled.

Today, I have advanced to healthier hole-fillers, like gardening, hiking and making a hobby out of healthy lifestyle choices.

Jesus is the cardiologist of our broken heart. There is a prophecy in Isaiah 61:1-3 declaring that a Savior will be born Who will open the eyes of the blind, heal the lame and bind up the broken hearted. In the Gospel of Luke, Jesus stands up in the temple, reads this prophecy and boldly proclaims that this prophecy is fulfilled in Him.

The Man of Sorrows, acquainted with grief, knows how to nurture, bind and heal your broken heart without a hot glue gun!

Heavenly Hope

What are your "go-to" crack fillers? We all have them! Are they ones that will bring healing and spiritual health?

But the fruit of the Spirit is love, joy, peace, long-suffering, kindness, goodness, faithfulness and self-control. Galatians 5:22, 23

There are many types of glue on the market. What type does the Holy Spirit want to use to fill those cracks?

With what does God promise to fill His People? (Psalm 81:10, Jeremiah 31:14)

_____

_____

_____

_____

_____

_____

_____

_____

_____

_____

_____

_____

_____

_____

Should Have, Could Have, Would Have

I confessed my transgressions to the Lord
and He forgave the guilt of my sins.
Psalm 32: 5

When Josiah took his life, we all thought of things we could have done differently that may have prevented his death. A mother whose small child drowned blamed herself for not bringing the water wings to the pool. A mother whose child died in a car accident on the way home from college said, "I should have insisted that he fly."

The "what if's" will kill you and get you stuck in your grief journey. We ultimately concluded that, yes, there were things we could have done differently, but God didn't show them to us! Given what we knew, we did what we thought was right at the time.

It is important, moms, to differentiate between regrets and guilt. Regret is something you wish you had or hadn't done, i.e., "I wish I had spent more time with my child." Guilt is something you actually did do wrong, i.e., "I knew my child was engaged in illegal activity and I didn't confront him."

For the regrets I suggest you write a letter to your child, listing and describing in detail each regret, ending with "I know you are not here to answer me, but will you please forgive me?"

Guilt, on the other hand, needs to be taken to the foot of the cross and left there. Nowhere in the Bible does it mention forgiving oneself. People will say, "I know God forgives me, but I can't forgive myself." This makes your court of justice higher than God's and keeps you in bondage. Satan is called the accuser of the brethren (Revelation 12:10) and he is at it day and night. For me, it's mostly at night!

The truth is yes, we are all guilty. The good news is that Jesus died not to just take away our sins but also the shame, blame and guilt of our sins. Our Pastor says, "There's no shame in our game!" And from Romans 8:1 *There is therefore now no condemnation for those who are in Christ Jesus.*

He is the I AM and we live in a "what is" world. Don't get stuck in a "what if" world. It is helpful for me to change my self-talk from: "If only I had ..." to: "I did the best I could, considering ..."

Heavenly Hope

For My thoughts are not your thoughts nor are your ways My ways, declares the Lord. For as the heavens are higher than the earth so are My ways higher than your ways and My thoughts than your thoughts! Isaiah 55:8, 9

Do you really know what difference it would have made if you had made different choices?

What casts out all fear of judgment? (I John 4:18)

Where is condemnation coming from? (Romans 8:1)

_____

_____

_____

_____

_____

_____

_____

_____

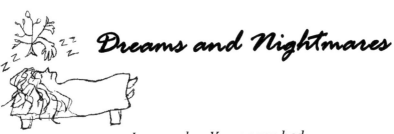 *Dreams and Nightmares*

I remember You on my bed;
I meditate on You in the night watches.
Psalm 63:6

Some moms have had significant dreams of their children. I've had a few, but like Shakespeare wrote in The Tempest: "When I waked, I cried to dream again!" The stark reality came when I awoke: "He's gone and never coming back!"

Nightmares and night terrors also are common for some moms. In Job 4:13-16 he describes very vividly his night terrors:

> Amid disquieting dreams in the night, when sleep falls
> on people, fear and trembling seized me and made all
> my bones shake. A spirit glided past my face and the
> hair on my body stood on end ... A form stood before
> my eyes and I heard a hushed voice.

The evil spirit basically went on to tell Job he was not righteous and God couldn't possibly care about him. Sound familiar?

Revelation 12:10 calls Satan "the accuser of the brethren." He is accusing them "day and night." I think it is significant that the Scripture adds "and night." It was then, in the dark quietness when the distractions of the day were gone, that Satan would come to me, showing me ways I screwed up and casting doubt on God's opinion of me.

Speaking of spirits, I also want to warn you moms of "channelers" and "spirit guides." A "channeler" contacted me shortly after Josiah died. She said she had a word from Josiah for me and would I like to meet up with her? Even though I desperately wanted a word from my son I said, "No thanks," because God condemns such practices in the Bible.

With perilous results, Saul, in 1 Samuel 28, went to a medium to conjure up Samuel from the grave. In Leviticus 20:6 God specifically told

His people that He would turn His face against those who turned their faces to (or consulted with) mediums and familiar spirits. He wants us to turn our faces to *Him*!

My eyes anticipate the night watches that I may meditate on Your Word. Psalm 119:148

Besides counting sheep, what have you found helpful when you cannot fall asleep?

The first few months after Josiah's death I listened to recorded Scripture verses at night to fall asleep. I would set a time limit and if I hadn't fallen asleep by, say 11:30, then I would take a sleeping pill, but I didn't choose to randomly take one every night.

When Satan accuses you at night what can you tell him?

For the accuser of the brethren, who accuses before our God day and night, has been hurled down! Hallelujah! Revelation 12:10

What is the ultimate fate of the accuser of the brethren?

How can we get Satan to leave us alone? (James 4:7)

Write Zechariah 3:1-5 and Luke 22:31, 32 on some card stock and read them when you need encouragement.

_____

_____

_____

_____

_____

_____

_____

Fear of Losing Another

That He might render powerless him who had the power of death,
that is, the devil, and might free those who through
the fear of death were subject to slavery all their lives.
Hebrews 2:14, 15

Shortly after Josiah died, sheer heart-stopping panic would overwhelm me every time I heard an ambulance or received a late-night call. Honestly, I still can struggle with the fear of losing "another sparrow."

It took so much work, prayer and effort to survive the loss of one that – at some level – my own survival is at stake should I lose another. Reality is that some moms lose more than one and some moms lose all.

Daily I walk with Chris who has lost all! She is a severely wounded warrior who is very courageous.

Bottom line? Everyone is going to die some time. All precious, loving human relationships will be parted by death and our worrying cannot add an hour to one's life. (Matthew 6:27)

Just months after Josiah died I received *the call.* My daughter had been projected through the back window of a rolled Bronco going 70 mph on I-70. She was on her way by ambulance to Swedish Hospital in Denver. The "cords of death" sought to strangle me (Psalm 18:4, 5), as we rushed to Denver. Fortunately she survived and since has gone on to survive melanoma and a gnarly bike accident that put her in a wheel chair for a month.

Another son was in the operating room under anesthesia for a completely shattered clavicle (on my birthday) when the power went out in the entire hospital. Panicked, I flew from the waiting room into the operating room itself, where they had an ambu-bag on him until the generator kicked in. He, too, survived.

Miracles, you say? Was it not just as much a miracle that our Josiah was taken up into eternity by angels? I have learned it is not mine to judge, which is the miracle.

I try not to hover over my kids as a helicopter mom or grandmother. But I still do. It's a false sense of holding the keys of life and death.

Do not be afraid. I am the first and the last, the Living One. I was dead and behold I am alive forevermore and I have the keys of death and of Hades. Revelation 1:17, 18

Who holds the keys to death and Hades? Would you want the keys that determine who dies when and how? Journal your thoughts as you consider this.

How is fear enslaving? (Romans 8:15, Hebrews 2:14, 15)

_____

_____

_____

_____

_____

_____

_____

_____

_____

_____

Will I Ever Laugh Again?

He will yet fill your mouth with laughter
and your lips with shouting.
Job 8:21

Shortly after Josiah died I had a startling realization: "I'll never laugh again!" No, really. I'll never experience hearty, belly-felt, cry-to-tears laughter. Like so many early grief thoughts, it broadsided me and sent me running to my wailing wall.

People who know me know I am all about fun and laughter. I've been told it's my spiritual gift to the body (not listed in Scripture, so don't look it up!).

BJD my sister and I rented a convertible and drove to the Florida Keys with the top down singing at the top of our lungs "Fun Fun Fun" by the Beach Boys (apologies to any introverts who can't relate).

Early guilt was associated with smiles and laughter – like: "Uh, Oh, I smiled at someone at the funeral. Did I just betray my son?" When rare times of pleasure came, I thought "How can I possibly be enjoying myself when my child died?"

When Abraham was told that barren Sarah – his wife would have a son at age 90, he hid his face and laughed (Genesis 17). When Sarah was told she would have a son, she too laughed, but her guilt made her quickly deny it. I picture the Angel of God smiling at her when He said, "Oh but you did laugh!"

Years later she birthed her baby. She named him Isaac. Guilt gone, his name means "laughter." After Isaac was born Sarah proclaimed, "God has made laughter for me; everyone who hears will laugh with me."

God will make laughter for you again. It may be a year or five years, but it *will* happen. When it does, you will always remember it.

Mine was with my friend, Cindy. We jumped into an ice-cold ocean-filled pool in March – to the shock and raised eyebrows of bystanders! Getting out we ran to the locker room only to discover there were no working showers or towels!

We tried to get our various body parts under the faucet in the sink to rinse off the salt water with the small trickle of warm water. I, being the shorter of the two of us, got my foot stuck up in the high sink, while hopping on the other foot. The more we laughed the harder it was to get it out. Falling on the bathroom floor, we laughed until we cried from more than just our eyes! It was such a welcomed release!

Heavenly Hope

Our mouth was filled with laughter and our tongue with joyful shouting. Then they said, "The Lord has done great things for us." Psalm 126:2

Have you had your "first laugh?" When was it? If not, can you foresee a day when this might occur? When it happens you will remember it!

Ecclesiastes 3:4 refers to a time *to laugh* and a time *to mourn*. Trust the seasons; winter is dark and bare but one can look up through the bare branches and see the stars!

_____

_____

_____

_____

_____

_____

_____

Wiped Away Tears

*For the Lamb in the center of the throne will be their Shepherd and
will guide them to springs of the water of life
and God will wipe away every tear from their eyes.*
Revelation 7:17

Well, precious sisters, we began with tears flooding into a bottle and look at our ending: The "wounded Lamb" becomes the Shepherd; like the Shepherd in Psalm 23, He guides us to "still waters" and gently, lovingly guides us to God to have our souls restored and our tears wiped away!

What a beautiful scene: God, Who could have prevented our child's death – and our pain – is standing by the Water of Life Springs, ready to wipe away every tear.

My sister currently resides at The Springs in Florida. The natural spring there is *always* crystal clear, *always* swarming with life, *always* the same perfect temperature. Consistency after chaos: still, refreshing water, after threatening tumultuous waves!

The Psalmist sings in Chapter 23 that in the huge, looming darkness, it was actually "Goodness" and "Mercy" who were following us all the days of our lives!

God – the same God who allowed our tears – wipes our tears, inviting us to feast with our children at the banqueting table under The Banner of Love! This is Heavenly Hope and Healing, moms!

He tends His flock like a shepherd; He gathers the lambs in his arms and carries them close to his heart; He gently leads those that have young. Isaiah 40:11

"Those that have young" are the mommy sheep. That's us!

Where is He carrying you and why would a lamb need to be carried?

Explore what the Bible says about the Lord being "your Shepherd." (Genesis 48:15, Genesis 49:24, Psalm 28:9, John 10:11-14)

Read Psalm 23 as if you are looking down on your life from Heaven. What is coming up behind you today? What lies before you?

_____

_____

_____

_____

_____

_____

_____

_____

_____

_____

_____

_____

_____

_____

_____

Good Grief!

Okay, sister survivors, you've worked hard and persevered to the end of this journal. Now I want to share a treasure we received in the darkness: an unexpected puzzle piece that made so much fit together. I hope it will encourage you.

Josiah's Special Message

In his painful dying moments, Josiah saw Jesus and wrote about it!

John and I found the note by his bed where he died. It had blood on it, but because we were in shock, the writing looked like that of a younger child, not a 15-year-old. I folded it up to examine later.

Several weeks later I had gotten the autopsy report back stating there was approximately a 15-minute lapse from the time he shot himself until the time he died. I cried, "Lord, can you tell me what happened during those moments?" I played Russian Roulette with my Bible, opening it at random and my eyes fell upon Ezekiel 16:6-12.

It is a message to Israel from God, but that morning it was for me:

> *... When I passed by you and saw you struggling in your own blood I said to you in your blood "live." ... It was a time for love, I spread my wing over you, I entered into a covenant with you, and you became Mine, says the Lord God ... I thoroughly washed off your blood and I anointed you with oil ... I clothed you in embroidered cloth ... and placed a beautiful crown on your head ...*

I breathed a prayer: "Thank you Lord for calling Josiah to real life! Thank you Lord for washing the blood from him and loving him and for placing a crown on the head of my boy-king."

That would have been enough but opening my bedside drawer to get a pen I discovered his note. Like the "Magic Eye" book, it all came into focus.

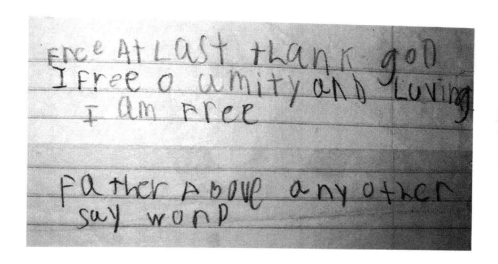

I knew now from Ezekiel that the word Josiah was waiting for God to say was, "live." Like dying Stephen and many of my Christian hospice patients, he was seeing Jesus in those fifteen minutes. God moved him to write what he saw as an encouragement for the surviving moms.

He wrote of the three main things that are so important to know about God: He is mighty, He is loving, and He is our Father. If He were mighty and not loving, that would not be good. If He were loving but not mighty, that would be okay, but not great. If He were mighty and loving but not my Father, that would not be good either. The special message is this: As wounded warriors He is all three to us, and He was all three to our precious fallen sparrows: Mighty, Loving and Father.

A Sparrow Story

I've been privileged to be a presenter at *Umbrella Ministries* conferences. This is a wonderful weekend conference for moms who are grieving the loss of their child:
www.umbrellaministries.com.

At the New Jersey Fall Conference I entered my room after helping decorate tables and there, sitting on my pillow, was a small sparrow. He looked at me, hopped unafraid around my room, out to the balcony rail, and then flew on his way.

In my room that evening I met with six other moms of suicide loss. There was one hesitant mom who told me it was too early for her to share anything. But when I shared about the sparrow being in the room, she said that *now she had to share...* As she was awaiting her ride to conference, she went out to fill the bird feeder. All the birds flew away except one. Amazed, she filled the feeder as he balanced on the edge. Then she actually reached out and stroked him with her finger.

The following morning another mom in our small group came up to me and said "Lynda, you won't believe this, but there was a sparrow on my bed this morning!"

God had my attention! I asked the front desk attendant and our housekeeper (of ten years) if they had ever heard of birds in the room and they both said "Never." Now I don't believe in "spirit guides" other than the Holy Spirit, or that these birds were our children, but I do believe the Heavens declare the glory of God and like Moses' burning bush, God was showing up that day.

That weekend I began noticing a common thread in the women's stories that I hadn't noticed at other conferences. In our small group, one child had jumped from a seventy foot crane, another jumped from the tenth story of a high rise, one of the speaker's sons jumped off the Coronado bridge. The next morning on a beach hike, two moms shared how both of their sons died falling off a balcony in Prague – two years apart. What are the odds?

God connected the dots. Jesus said that when a sparrow falls to the ground, your Father knows it.

Whether your child fell to his death, drowned, died of medical causes, drug overdose, murder, miscarriage, or stillborn – the message is the same: Jesus wants you to know that your loving Father is not some distant impersonal God. He is very aware that your child died and He cares!

Preview from

A Sparrow Sings

Renewing Your Joy as
Your Sparrow's Song is Sung

An upcoming Devotional
in finding purpose through the pain of losing a child

I sing because I'm happy, I sing because I'm free, for His eye is on the sparrow, and I know He watches me.

Your Seed's Potential

*Unless a grain of wheat falls
into the ground and dies it remains alone.
But if it dies it produces much grain!*
John 12:24

Parable? Riddle? A dead seed, fallen into the cold earth produces much fruit!

Our kids loved reading Frog and Toad books. One particular adventure found Frog and Toad planting and watering some seeds. Anticipation was followed by discouragement as they daily checked on their seeds and found nothing but black dirt! Finally one day, a small green sprout of hope ...

The seed of your child's death can produce an entire field of grain! You may not even imagine this now as you stare at the black earth and feel that sense of anticipation continually eclipsed by disappointment. But I've seen it happen over and over again.

Tears water our seed. God adds His Son-shine and *with time*, miracles happen.

Everyone's crop will appear unique, but the essence of grain is that it nourishes someone!

Our friends, The Moritz's, started Breanna's House of Joy for orphaned girls in Thailand in honor of their precious Breanna Joy, who was killed in a car accident. Other moms have formed anti-bullying groups. One started a lifeguard awareness group to prevent drownings. Another opened a ranch for girls who are sex trafficked. My hiking friend, Chris, went on to become a Stephen Minister and now volunteers at a home for Alzheimer patients.

Your crop doesn't have to be huge like theirs. It could be as simple as helping with *GriefShare*, or taking another hurting mom to coffee... and I'm just saying, that sometimes our own seed needs to die to self in order to become fruitful.

To learn more on cultivating a garden from your fallen seed,
please join me in our soon-to-come devotional:
A Sparrow Sings,
Allow your Fallen Sparrow to teach you
to fly and to sing again!

For more of Lynda's Poems and Artwork
or to contact Lynda-visit:
www.HeavenlyHopeAndHealing.com/sparrow

Lynda@HeavenlyHopeAndHealing.com

My Prayer

Thanks for sharing these 40 visits together. My prayer for you is that you have found some Heavenly Hope and Healing in your journey and have deepened in your knowledge of the Man of Sorrows!

Heavenly Hope Support Group Guide

To be used in conjunction with
A Sparrow Falls

Creating and Guiding a Support Group for Grieving Moms

Gathering a Village of Grieving Moms

Leader's Guide

Group Guidelines

Hands on Activities

Conversation Starters

Scriptural Hope and Prayers

GATHER A VILLAGE

Creating and Guiding a Support Group for Grieving Moms

To be used in conjunction with *A Sparrow Falls* Devotional Guide

LET'S GET STARTED – IT'S AS EASY AS 1, 2, 3 !

Starting a *Heavenly Hope* Support Group is a beautiful way to honor your child's death and encourage other grieving moms. Not only will you be fulfilling the commission to "Comfort others with the comfort you have received..." II Corinthians 1:4, but as you encourage others you just may discover your own *Heavenly Healing* along the way!

STEP 1 Gather your Tribe

Size doesn't matter! It may be as small as two or three of you in a coffee shop or perhaps a larger gathering of grieving moms at your church.

Social media, local children's hospitals, counseling groups, schools, newspapers, even local news stations are all good places to seek out and reach hurting moms.

Ask God to bring moms to you and then put on your "mom antennas."

Contact potential participants sharing the "Mission and Purpose" of the group: *Heavenly Hope and Healing* is a faith-based program that provides hope and community for grieving moms. It is to be used in conjunction with *A Sparrow Falls* Devotional Guide.

STEP 2 Formulate and Communicate *The Plan*

Determine your time, place and expected length of sessions. For example: "We will meet once a week for 8 weeks on Thursday nights from 7-8:30 pm at the church."

Your times and places may be completely different, depending on everyone's needs and preferences.

STEP 3 Familiarize yourself with this "The Leader's Guide "

There are 40 *A Sparrow Falls* devotions from which to choose. If you have only eight weeks of class you will need to pick your favorite eight chapters. The hands-on group activities in "The Leader's Guide" correspond to the Devotional chapters and *Heavenly Hope* questions found in *A Sparrow Falls.* Moms should read the assigned devotional prior to coming to class. The *Heavenly Hope* questions will be discussed along with moms participating in the group activities during your Support Group session.

Several of the sessions will require a *small* amount of preparation and financial investment, such as purchasing balloons, markers etc; many of them require no preparation other than prayer. Do what fits your style.

SUGGESTIONS for GROUP TIME

Begin with a prayer

Each session should begin with a brief prayer or you may read the following prayer:

God, our Loving Father, wrap Your arms around each mom in our group as we meet today; Jesus, Man of Sorrows, bring understanding to each of us, as One who has been through pain and suffering: Holy Spirit, be the Comforter that You are, to each mom today. In Jesus' name, Amen.

Keep the group discussion focused and hopeful

The goal is to have moms leave with more *Heavenly Hope* than they arrived. Keep conversations centered on the topic and Scriptures.

Encourage moms to be aware that each person needs to be allowed time to share. Frequently, I will start by asking the extroverts to raise their hands, followed by the introverts raising their hands. Then I ask the extroverts to look around and be sure they are allowing the introverts time to share each week.

If your group is large or there is a continued issue with one person monopolizing the conversation every time, implement a "talking stick." This is a stick that is passed around as each person is asked to answer the question. If a mom chooses to remain silent she can simply pass the stick to the next mom.

Allow room for the Holy Spirit to show up! If one mom is especially sad or new to her loss, take time to gather around her, lay your hands on her and pray for her.

Ending your session

Honor everyone's time by ending on schedule; if one mom needs added attention dismiss the others, then visit and pray with that particular mom.

If you have access to technology, play a song from our *Music with Marilyn* page found at: heavenlyhopeandhealing.com/sparrow.

End the session with a prayer of thanks to God, lifting up any special concerns brought up in the session and praying encouragement for each mom as she continues on her journey during the upcoming week.

A tradition with *Umbrella Ministries* at the end of each conference is a yellow balloon-release ceremony. You may want to consider this when your support group time has come to an end. Yellow, bio-degradable, helium balloons can be purchased and brought to the class. Each mom writes a message to her child on the balloon. Moms gather outside in an open area with music playing and they all release the balloons together.

Year-Round Support

Holidays are especially hard on moms. This is what we are doing in our area:

Mother's Day Tea

This can be a brunch or tea the Saturday before Mother's Day, honoring moms and acknowledging their child/children. Since it is Spring, a

Butterfly Release ($3.00 per butterfly) or passing out seed packets may be appropriate.

Holiday Survival Christmas Luncheon

Moms gather for a potluck luncheon. After lunch we make ornaments using empty glass or plastic fillable bulbs. We decorate the outside with glitter and trim, write a message to our child on paper rolled up like a scroll and place it in the ornament; we then fill the remainder of the ball with gold and silver garland. They are beautiful!

For continued support we recommend joining a GriefShare group, www.griefshare.org and/or attending a
Journey of the Heart Conference: www.Umbrellaministries.com

Better yet, bring your village to our Colorado Conference: Heavenlyhopeandhealing.com

Thank you for reaching out to other moms. It is a *most beautiful of ways* to honor a child's death! Love to you all!

Lynda Shelhamer
Mother of Josiah

Lynda@heavenlyhopeandhealing.com

Leader's Guide

Treasures in the Darkness

Action:

Purchase and distribute "Gold Coins." These can
be plastic gold coins, (Dollar Store), foil covered chocolate coins, or
Sacajawea $1.00 gold coins purchased from the bank. Instruct the
moms that the coins are to be placed by their bedside to remind them
to look for "treasures in their darkness."

Discussion:

Use 3 words to describe your darkness.
What does it mean to you that Jesus sits with you in your darkness?

Tears in a Bottle

Action:

Bring at least three bottles of different sizes and colors to class. Ask
moms which bottle they most identify with and why?

Discussion:

What title would you give to your Book of Tears?
Why would God choose to wipe away our tears rather than prevent
them?

Mary's Perfume

Action:

Just prior to class, spray your favorite perfume around the classroom
until it is noticeable. (Be sensitive if any mom has allergies; you may
want to use essential oils.)

Discussion:

Do you feel your child's death to be a "total waste?" What does it mean to you to pour out your *tear-infused perfume at Jesus' feet?*

Loosened Sack Cloth

Action:

Instruct moms, during the week, to bring their most uncomfortable clothing item to the group; have them describe to the group why they find it so uncomfortable.

Discussion:

Describe how your garment of sackcloth feels; can you ever imagine it being totally gone or just "loosened?" Why do we always carry scraps of sackcloth with us?

Ground Zero

Action:

Look at and print Lynda's picture of the war scene at www.heavenlyhopeandhealing.com/sparrow. Who do the various figures represent in your life? Describe how they assisted you as the "victim."

Discussion:

Which of the "moment of death" terms do you most identify with? Night of Nightmares, The Crash Site, Ground Zero, Moment of Terror? Other?

Have you shared the details with anyone or journaled them? Why or why not?

Victim or Victor?

Action:

Draw a road on a poster board. Draw a directional sign pointing two opposite ways. Label one way "Victim" and one way "Victor."

Discussion:

Ask moms which road they feel they are currently taking. Can you imagine your child's death as becoming a "defining moment" in your life in a positive way?

My Upside Down World

Action:

Pass a ball of yarn around the room and have each mom tangle it a little more as it comes her way. Have it go around at least 3 times.

Discussion:

Does this ball of tangled yarn feel like your new world?
Have you experienced the sensation of being lost or disorientated? When or where?

Anger -- Where Do I Put it?

Action:

Give each mom an inflated balloon and a marker. Have her write people or things that generate anger with regards to her child's death, e.g., cancer, car accident. Multiple things can be written on each balloon. Together, put your balloons on the floor and stomp on them until they burst!

Discussion:

Share someone or something that triggers your anger, without mentioning names. Are you comfortable expressing your anger to God? Why or why not?

Just Breathe

Action:

Did you know that babies breathe with their stomach muscles? Somehow we've lost that as we have gotten older! Have moms place their hand flat across their abdomen, inhale deeply, expanding their stomach out as far as they can without raising their shoulders. Take at least 20 breaths like this with eyes closed, breathing in through the nose and out through the mouth. Good exercise to do when stressed.

Discussion:

Can you identify with the "loss of breath" sensation?
What have you found helpful in these situations?

The Grand Canyon:

Action:

Look at the canyon picture (heavenlyhopeandhealing.com/sparrow) Which ledge best describes where you are in your grief journey?

Discussion:

Have you ever climbed something steep? Describe the similarities in sensations with the effort it takes to climb out of the "Canyon of Grief!"

I Thought God was Good!

Action:

Bring something tasty to class for each mom. Psalms 34:8 says, "Taste and see that the Lord is good ..." Explain how you can hold it, look at it, smell it and feel it, but until you *taste it* you really don't know if it's good. How is that similar to the Lord's goodness according to this verse?

Discussion:

In the book, *The Chronicles of Narnia,* the child is asked, "Is Aslan, the Lion, safe?" The child replies: "Oh no! He's not safe at all, but He *is* good!" Do you think there is a difference between God being *safe* and God being *good*? Explain.

Holidays and Significant Events

Action:

Pass out blank birthday cards to each mom. Have her write her child's name and *heavenly* birth date on the envelope. Inside the card have her write a message to her child.

Discussion:

Share what you have done to acknowledge your child on a significant date.

The Court Room

Action:

As the defendant, make notes of your key points as to why God should not have taken your child.

Discussion:

State "your case" to the group as to why God shouldn't have taken *your* child.
Be sure to reiterate Job's final verdict from the verses. Who would you rather have sitting on the Judgment Seat - you or God?

My Secret Garden

Action:

Bring a flower for each mom. I like Star-Gazer Lilies because they are crazy fragrant!

Discussion:

Share your "go-to-place" when you are sad, lonely or scared. Would you consider sharing this place with a friend this week?

The Anchor and the Hope Rope

Action:

Bring six inch sections of large, thick cut-up rope from the hardware store and a sharpie marker. Have each mom write on the rope: "Hope–Hebrews 6:19."

Discussion:

How has grief been like drowning for you? Name at least four words you find in Hebrews 6:19 that describe your anchor.

Music's Healing Power

Action:

Play the song *Welcome Home* by Michael W. Smith.

Google and read the history of the song *It is Well with My Soul.* Pass out the words to each mom. Using *YouTube*, look up the song by Bethel Music or another source and have moms sing along at the close of the class.

Discussion:

Is there a song that has especially touched you since your child has died? Sing it! No, not really. Share why....

Don't Lose Your Child and Your Spouse

Action:

If you have a spouse, share your own story of how grief has affected your relationship with your spouse. Be sensitive to moms who are single or divorced and tell them they can refer to other relationships in their life.

Discussion:

Has grief drawn you closer or farther apart as a couple? If you are divorced or not married, how have your other relationships changed?

Comparing Wounds

Action:

Have moms look at Lynda's picture of the girl on crutches (www.heavenlyhopeandhealing.com/sparrow). Which stage of grief do you most identify with today?

Discussion:

Is it hard for you not to compare your pain with others? How do other people's "child celebrations" make you feel?

Missing Puzzle Pieces

Action:

Bring a small puzzle to class. Have moms work on the puzzle together. Hide 3 or 4 pieces in your pocket, never to be revealed!

Discussion:

How does it feel not to be able to complete this puzzle? What part or parts of your puzzle are missing? Do you have any "secret pieces" you would like to pull out of your pocket and place on the table tonight? No obligations, of course!

Beam Me Up, Scotty

Action:

Bring magazines. Have moms cut out pictures of somewhere they would rather be other than **here!**

Discussion:

Can you identify with this statement? "It's not like the grieving mom wants to die, she just doesn't want to be *here*." Have moms explain how this might reflect their feelings.

The Refiner's Fire

Action:

Bring small votive candles for each mom to light, representing *her fire*. Keep the candles burning during class discussion time.

Discussion:

What is the difference between "fool's gold" and 24K gold? Do you feel that your child's death is some kind of punishment for you? Be honest!

Where Was God When Josiah Died?

Action:

On a piece of paper, draw a picture of your child (can be a stick figure). Next, draw something that represents God in your picture. Place the picture of God as close or distant to your child as you feel He was at the time of your child's death.

Discussion:

What do you think may have been happening on the heavenly side while your child was passing? Do you have anything to indicate that God may have been with your child during this passing?

Expectations of Self

Action:

Bring a yard stick to class. Have moms express where they currently see their expectations of self.

Discussion:

What is one self-expectation you can let go of today? Celebrate this!

Expectations of Others

Action:

Have moms share "stupid things" people have said to them. To lighten things up, have class vote on "worst in category."

Using a yardstick, have each mom express where her expectations of others are.

Discussion:

Has someone said, done, or *not done* something that has caused you to feel resentment? Are there activities around you that create resentment in you?

Memories

Action:

Have moms bring or wear something they might have to honor their child, i.e. locket, photo T-shirt, etc.

Bring a poster board and thumb tacks to class and have moms post one or two pictures of their children on the board.

Discussion:

Share a "bittersweet" memory you have of your child or an aspiration that will never come to fruition.

The Shadow of Death Valley

Action:

Ahead of time, cut out a cardboard bird. Using a sheet and flashlight, practice making the bird look much larger than it is; then show it to the moms at class.

Discussion:

Describe some shadows that are scary to you. What's your "big bird" on the sheet?

Your Wailing Wall

Action:

Designate and label a wall in your group room as the Wailing Wall. Holding hands, walk together to the wall and groan together. There is a place in the literal wall in Jerusalem where people write a prayer on a small piece of paper, roll it up and press it into the cracks on the wall. Have moms do the same with tape.

Discussion:

Do you prefer to grieve alone or with others? Do you have a place where you can wail?

Jesus Loves Me, This I Know

Action:

Print out all the lyrics to *Jesus Loves Me,* giving a copy to each mom. Let the words penetrate your hearts as you sing it together.

Discussion:

How has Jesus shown His love for you? Be specific!

What is the difference between *Jesus Loves Me, This I Know* and *Jesus Knows Me, This I Love?*

Why Me? Why My Child?

Action:

Place a bucket or large bowl approximately 10ft. from the moms. Have moms wad up paper into a ball. On the count of three, have them toss their ball into the bowl. Some balls may make it into the bowl; others will not.

Discussion:

Was it a random event or the Providence of God that your child didn't survive until old age?

Can you think of something that maybe God, in His mercy, might have been sparing your child from?

Embracing a New Normal

Action:

Have moms arrange a "coffee date" with someone new to them in the class. Instruct them to bring pictures of their children to share with each other.

Discussion:

What new friends or activities have you discovered or developed in your life since your child passed?

Lonely and Abandoned

Action:

Give each mom a piece of black construction paper and white chalk. Have moms draw something that represents their loneliness.

Discussion:

Has your child really abandoned you? Describe your "winter," using your five senses.

My Broken Shell Collection

Action:

Bring some broken shells to class (I have found them at thrift stores). Hand a shell to each mom. Have the moms hold their shell up to a bright light and describe the patterns, textures and colors they are seeing.

Discussion:

The largest, stormiest waves bring the best treasures to shore. What do you feel as you think about this in relation to your child's death?

Is My Child in Heaven?

Action:

At the end of the class, share your own assurance of salvation. Ask the moms if anyone else is comfortable sharing her "testimony."

Discussion:

What did you think of the life raft illustration?

Really? An Attitude of Gratitude?

Action:

Purchase journals or notebooks for each woman. Have moms number 1-25 down the side of the first page. Encourage them to return to the next session with 25 things they have been grateful for during this time.

Discussion:

Share three things you have been grateful for this past week.

My Broken Heart

Action:

Bring coloring sheets to class with a picture of a large, cracked heart on each sheet, leaving space in between the cracks for writing. Have moms write in the cracks what their crack fillers might be including some healthy and some not so healthy ones.

Discussion:

Share your heart picture, if you are comfortable.

Should Have, Could Have, Would Have

Action:

Bring a large cut-out cardboard cross. Have each mom draw two columns on a piece of paper. Title one column "Guilt" and one column "Regret." Have the moms list some of their *guilts* and *regrets* in each column. Have the moms pray and ask God to forgive them and remove their guilt for the things listed in the "Guilt" column. Cut the paper in half and pin the list of *guilts* to the cardboard cross facing backwards (so no one sees the lists). Discuss how any guilt associated with their child's death has been removed by the cross of Christ. Destroy lists at the end of class. Have each mom write a brief letter to her child expressing her *regrets* for things that she may have done or may have neglected to do.

Discussion:

Describe the difference between guilt and regret. Share an illustration of each, or your own guilt vs. regret, if you are comfortable.

Dreams and Nightmares

Action:

Set the timer for 3 minutes. Have each mom draw a sketch of a dream or nightmare she may have had since her child died. Explain that art talent has nothing to do with this drawing, thus the short time period!

Discussion:

Ask moms to share a dream or a nightmare they may have had since their child's death. If they haven't had any, that's okay; some moms never do. Discuss with the moms what the setting of their ideal dream might be.

Fear of Losing Another

Action:

Bring keys to class, labeled *Keys Of Death*. Hanging them out of reach, have moms grab for them.

Discussion:

Does it bring you comfort or anger that Jesus, not you, holds the keys to life and death?

Will I Ever Laugh Again?

Action:

Find your funniest Internet video and bring it to show the class.

Discussion:

Do you feel guilty when you laugh or are having a good time? Have moms share the first time they laughed after their child passed, if they remember it.

Wiped Away Tears

Action:

Distribute pretty purse-sized tissue packages to each mom. Have moms write "Revelation 21:4" on them with markers.

Discussion:

Who is the Great Tear-Wiper... Jesus or God? What part does Jesus play in the Tear Wiping Ceremony?

Acknowledgments

I want to thank my friends with an eye for detail and a heart for ministry: Ellen Graham, Kathleen Nalley and my sister, Lois Wesley all of whom proof read my book ad infinitum. If there are still any literary errors remaining, please don't tell us!

My patient and ever-enduring husband, John, who finalized the final copy of the tenth "final" copy of this manuscript! Thanks Hon!

Chris Volberding who, despite the passing of both her children, offered freely her graphic talents to escort my "little girl graphics" to the corner of each page.

To Julie Bergeron, who helped me move my pain from the inside onto paper with our very amateur art therapy sessions.

To my amazing kids: Johnny, Amber and Zak, who chose not to turn their backs on the God Who could have prevented Josiah's death. I love you to heaven and back!

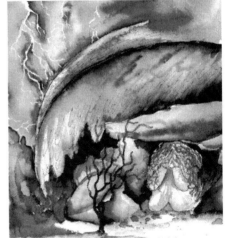

To Daisey Catchings, founder of *Umbrella Ministries*, who invited me and so many other moms under her umbrella of love.

Finally, I'm drop on my knees grateful, to the Sparrow-Holder who taught me how to breathe and sing again.

About the Author

Whether it's embracing a goat in India, inviting a homeless man over for a shower or just loving on those around her, Lynda Shelhamer does it with courage and compassion. Her mantra is to *receive life, live life and give life.*

As a Registered Nurse she has done it all: treating bear maulings in Alaska, giving tsunami relief in India, delivering babies on remote islands. Her last nine years as an RN were in the field of hospice care. She states: "I use to help people die now I help people live!"

Her life resume includes: married to John for 41 years, mom to four amazing children (one who resides in heaven) and three photo-hogging grandchildren.

Lynda calls Colorado "home" where she hikes and bikes in the mountains and, when feeling Aboriginal, paddleboards the lakes.

She and her husband work with *GriefShare* and *Umbrella Ministries.* She is founder of *Heavenly Hope and Healing Conferences and Ministry.* Currently she works and plays in the field of plant-based nutrition with *The Juice Plus Company.*

Her vision is to help women realize they are God's Divas and that He is crazy in love with them!

P.S She's also a Bible Study Nerd and wants you to become one too!

Made in the USA
San Bernardino, CA
21 March 2018